Professor and the Virgin Nymphet

Sophia

Published by Sophia, 2024.

PROFESSOR AND THE VIRGIN NYMPHET

First edition. March 5, 2024.

Copyright © 2024 Sophia.

ISBN: 979-8227578075

Written by Sophia.

Table of Contents

Chapter 1

The professor and the virgin nymphet First day

Love? What love? It is not by loving somebody that I was allowed in one of the best University of California.

I believe that the love is a distraction. That which likes becomes the hostage of somebody who can or not take care of his heart, but most of the time, the love destroys it.

I never wanted to be in this position, of fear of creating an emotional dependence with respect to somebody. I am called Céline, I am 18 years old and I am virgin.

Not that somebody ever tried to lay down me, but I do not think that I should give it to no matter whom. I am white, I have the green eyes, I have freckles and my hair is naturally russet-red. I draw the attention of the boys everywhere where I go and I continue to be badgered by them, which created a kind of defense in me.

Certain guys call me a girl of ice, others call me a dumb, and actually, I am only one girl ready to protect his heart. I am unmarried by choice. The day when I decided to leave with somebody, it put its hands on my centres the first week of appointment, and when I asked him to stop, it said to me that the buddies had sexual relationships, and that we should have sexual relationships, and when I decided to break, it had the audacity to treat me the ice-cold one.

I is not ice-cold, it is right which I do not treat the sex with banality. Today, it is my first day of school, in the courses of right, I want to be a lawyer like my parents, not because they forced me, but since I developed a love for this trade. In fact, it is the only reliable love.

As of my arrival at the university, I paid attention to all the girls, equipped very well, super made up, with gigantic heels, and much of them went as if they were on a podium.

Not that I under-was equipped, but I was not equipped either for the fashion shows. I sought my room, when a man passed in front of me, his odor impregnated my nostrils. It was white, large, male, had the rather young air and had a smile angelica. Its hair was very neat and it had a perfect goatee. Whereas it went in the corridor, much of girls went with him, calling it scented, beautiful and another called it a sexy professor.

- Thus it is a teacher? How much libertinage. I thought.

It is undeniable, it is very sexy, but apparently, it is a womanizer, and it is precisely this type of man who gives me desire for remaining unmarried. It stopped and chattered with girls, and I continued my research in the part, until I stop in front of one of them.

- It is that one. Before I enter, the professor womanizer also arrived in the same part.

Certain girls who were inside the part started to leave to greet it, and I had to move away me to avoid being trampled.

As soon as I entered, there were many boys and few girls, because the others were with the door kissing the professor. I sought a place where to sit me, where I could follow the course perfectly. Little by little, the students entered and sat down, I did not include/understand quite simply how they knew it then, if we were still in first half of the year, the room should be only for the first-year students.

I looked at my paper and I asked the girl beside me if I were in the good part. "You Slacken, there are many veterans here who repeat in his article, I am one". Thus, he was explained why they knew it already.

They spent so much time to dredge it that they forgot some to pay attention in class. "Hello the children, I am called Kyle, but everyone calls me Ky. I am constitutional law professor, and I hope that you can see me like one of your friends, not only like one professor, and I am here to solve all your doubts. I see that we have many new faces here, then are welcome.

The girls seniors started to applaud and the first-year students followed without really including/understanding why they received a smacking.

PROFESSOR AND THE VIRGIN NYMPHET

I was held in mine, not wanting to believe that this applause was for the professor.

Continuation for what? I made not head and I raised the eyes towards him, and I was surprised when I saw that it fixed me. People ceased applauding, and it looked at the class and thanked them, then again towards me, as if it analyzed me.

- Oh, save to me. You want that I applaud too? I thought. I looked at the ground and I laughed at my own thought when he spoke to me.

Kyle: Are hello, how you called? I looked at it and answered without fear.

- Celine.

Kyle: Do you want to share the reason of the pleasure with the class?

- Afflicted professor, but I have freedom to laugh without having to give explanations to somebody.

At the same time, the buzz started in the class.

Kyle: You are right, just like I have the right to teach you or not, can you please withdraw yourself.

- I will not withdraw myself as much as you me will not have given a plausible justification of it.

What will you say in the direction? Who didn't let me attend your course because I laughed in the middle of nowhere, or was the reason as I did not applaud you? The atmosphere was tended inside the classroom and the professor was completely insensitive.

- No justification? Eh well, then I remain, and you can make your please run, because I came here to study, it was not to inflate your ego. It looked around him in the part, then returned towards me.

Kyle: Of agreement Miss Céline, I drop this one because we did not have time yet to know us, perhaps that when you know me better, you will be more receptive and polished.

- I am only interested to know your subject, professor and not you. I noticed a light smile with the corner of his mouth, and its glance traversed all my body, it moved towards my chair, under the attentive glance of the pupils, and spoke to me with the ear.

Kyle: It is what we will see Miss Celine. It turned me the back and continued its course, while I felt my skin to crawl.

Chapter 2

The professor and the virgin nymphet Question of honor

I am called Kyle, I am 27 years old, I am unmarried and I teach the constitutional law in the University of California.

My life is animated from all points of view. When I am not at the university to teach, I am in evenings and clubs, and the majority of my companies are students of the university itself.

I know that for much, this relation teacher-raises is contrary with ethics, but nobody forever taken me along to the council, and the pupils like me especially the coeds.

My file is impeccable, and it is already the second consecutive year which I receive the title of better professor. I can that the students throw themselves on me, always want to take a cone, and I am not hypocritical by saying that I do not like that, some are really hot, and I even left with some among them, but nothing which would make me lose the concentration in my work.

While speaking about my personal life, I do not like the serious relations, and I do not remain either with a woman more twice, I like to be satisfied sexually, and in the sex, all is allowed, but I find with difficulty somebody who has the same fetish like me. I do not run after the women, they run after me, and my speciality is to wet their breeches.

I like to be put at the challenge, even if I know that I gain all the challenges which the women propose to me, they play, play hard, and I claim that they are it really, but finally, it is me which feel the taste of the victory.

Each six-month period, I go to the university, prepared to see a group women to stop my way, with their extravagant low neckline, practically rubbing their centres on my face, I must always be able early not to put myself late for my course. Some are obsessed so much by me, that they take bombs in my matter right to continue to follow courses with me, because I teach only with the first-year students or redoubling.

In the following six-month periods, there are other professors.

I am thus accustomed to having a high degree of attention, and anything else that returns to me curiously badly at ease.

Although that generally does not occur, until today, when a new pupil treated me like a "person" in my class. It already drew my attention because of the color of its hair, it of russet-red is coppered, its skin is white and its lips and its cheeks are very pink, and it wore a small dress violet, which emphasized its centres well, and the freckles on its face, they made it resemble one girl more that it was not it really, giving the impression of innocence.

It is not innocent whole. She laughed me with the nose and snobé me without shame, while offending to me in front of all the room. I even tried to drive out it part, but the girl is coed in right, it used all the reasonable arguments to prevent me to make it leave the part.

She did not need even more to study, she was completely ready to be an at the same time defense counsel and prosecutor.

I never met such a situation, of confrontation with a coed who was not even authorized to meet.

She did not look at me with desire like the others, she launched me cold glances and of judgment. I tried to be friendly and comprehensible, because it was its first day of school, but it was arrogant and impolite and made me understand that the only thing which interested it was my subject. I felt that there was a double direction in its speech, it is as if she wanted me to only tell that nothing me as a man interested it, my class.

I felt extremely badly at ease and at the same time put at the challenge. This girl did not know of what she thought when she decided to confront me. I advanced towards it, leaving a smile taquin, and spoke to him with the ear.

PROFESSOR AND THE VIRGIN NYMPHET

- It is what we will see, Miss Celine. I was diverted, feeling my cock already to palpitate, I went behind my office, I sat down on the chair and I waited until it is calmed. I did not dare any more to look at it, if there were a thing which this girl could make, it were me to destabilize.

And I will not let pass. Like the others, it carried also breeches wet for me. It is a question of honor of putting a term at the arrogance of this nymphet.

Its she-cat must be so pink and tight, that will be a true challenge to be around it without imagining it overlapping me and begging me to kiss it.

It is generally as that the women are for me, it will not be different with this girl. I want to see it starting again to coldly look at me and with me snober after I made it groan in an unverifiable way.

At the end of the course, I tightened the pupils in my arms and I embraced them on the cheek as usual. As soon as Céline left, I called it.

- Miss Céline? She looked at me and blew without too much patience. I could to him fesser the bottom after that.

- Which daring girl, I thought. Celine: There' does it have a professor with problem?

- Ouais, it is you the problem. Which arrogant manner to treat your professor.

Celine: Afflicted, tomorrow, I will bring a red carpet to you so that you steps above Mister.

- Lord nothing, calls me you. I am not so old, I am enough old to be your boyfriend.

Celine: You are enough old to be my grandfather, and I do not leave with seniors, now if you want to excuse me well, I must go to eat something before the next course.

She turned me the back and I was once again without voice.

- How this girl can be so shameless and unbearable like that? Grandmother? I am only 27 years old. I spent all the day to be thought of it, with the way in which it used words against me, with the way in which it behaved. If the first day, it already did me that, I do not want to even imagine what the remainder of the six-month period will resemble.

- Celine, Celine, you do not lose to wait. You me pays.

Chapter 3

The professor and the acid virgin nymphet Humor

To have the goose flesh for somebody who threatens me, even indirectly, is something again for me. "It is what we will see"... what it did want to say with that? He wants really to intimidate me.

It was disgusted that I do not dribble on him like the majority of these girls. I saw it sat behind the office without showing any reaction, it looked at me more, it passed all the class to be made as so nothing was.

- If this professor thinks that I am like these here desperate, it is mistaken. I hate the arrogant man and the womanizer. When its course was finally finished, I rose to see whether I could obtain something to eat. I did not even cross the door, it called me.

- Doesn't this type have any to make me enough shit? I thought. When I asked which was the problem, it had the base to say that the problem, it was me, that the way in which I treated it was arrogant. Then I said that I would bring a red carpet.

As if that were not enough, he even said me to call it you and not Sir, that it was not so old and that it was enough old to be my boyfriend. It was completely annoyed when I said that it was enough old to be my grandfather and that I did not leave with elderly.

I turned the back to him and left it in the shit, because I do not have any patience for a man who thinks that it has least control on the women. I am Master of me. I do not need any man to dictate what I owe or do not have to make, which I owe or do not have to say. As soon as I sat down with table to eat, a woman sat down beside me. "Isn't Hello, I am called Emily, you are Celine? I was in the classroom when you struck the professor."

- With don't the Emily pleasure, say to me that you are one of his defenders?

Emily: I had practice to make it, but when I saw at which point it was a womanizer, I ended up releasing taken.

- Choices Excel then.

Emily: It is a very selective guy, he saw surrounded women, but little of them succeeded in putting it at the bed.

- Does it remain with the students here? It is not prohibited?

Emily: Not here, unless there is a charge of harassing, but does it of it is him which is badgered.

- Then it is explained why it feels like the king of the jungle, this group of girls the met at ease to think that it is it really, I do not know honestly what they see in him.

Emily: Will Oh, you say to me that you do not find either it nice?

- It is beautiful, but not my kind. I do not love the guy which courts and which is frivolous. Pretty face which I can find on any corner.

Emilie: Ouais, you are right. Then I go to my next course, I am to the second half-year, I were only in your room because I had a bomb in his chair. Until later.

- Until. This guy is worse than than I thought. Not only he likes to be the center of the attention, but he makes himself also difficult for the women who have the fancy for him.

- Oh, have a holy patience. I said myself. Will he think that I am like them? Is this if it is for that he said that to my ear? In an attempt to convert me with the charm which he accurately does believe to have? Because if it is the intention, it badly will fall from horse. I am not conceited like him.

I do not need to be the center of the attention to feel me beautiful and desired. I did not see it a remainder of the day, which was marvellous for me.

Eh well, I did not have any more patience for him.

I returned insane to the house to take a shower and to try to remove me from the stress that this professor me because. I had still not forgotten his threat.

In fact, I spent all the day to be thought of each word which he said. Since when do have I to better know you? Is this the law that I like it? It will know with which it plays, I know exactly how to put it at its place.

I do not work, I go just to the university. Then during my spare time, when I do not study, I make sport, I adore to run and make bicycle. But this day, I decided not to do it, I had a whole plan at the head.

A plan which I would put into practice the following day. I travelled by my car and I went to buy a red carpet, I bought approximately two meters. It was small and fine, could be folded and would return perfectly in my bag.

Does the teacher want to be the center of attention? Thus I would make him feel this way.

It is not that I am arrogant, as it said, I hate just whoever tries to impose something to me.

I have a sour mood, and he is not enough man to face my sourness, which I appreciated. It is him which needs to better know me before thinking that I should follow it everywhere like insane, despaired of sex.

I never let myself carry by anyone. I have a total control on my feelings and my reactions. I am led by myself, it is me which decides if somebody draws my attention or not. I am not easy to handle and Maria does not go either with the others. A person must make to have my attention much more and to be a womanizer does not certainly form part of the requirements required to have it.

The evening when my parents returned of work, the first thing that they asked over my first day of school, if that had been well or not, if the professors were really qualified.

If they knew that the qualification of my constitutional law professor is the women and the sex, they certainly would see the senior the following day. I started to find my thoughts amusing.

Dad: What makes you laugh young girl? Why my father did ask that? At this point in time I laughed even more.

- Afflicted dad, it is the second time that it is asked me why I laugh.
Father: And which required in first?

- Ah, just a friend who made a joke idiot lied.

Father: Be wary of the distractions my love. he says by embracing me on the cheek. Mom: Then you show me what you studied today, of agreement?

- OK Maman. My parents are not caught any with me, they just help me for my studies and I adore that. After having dined, I went in my room and I prepared my bag for the following day. After having taken a shower and to be to me brushed the teeth, I finally could lengthen me in my bed and sleep of the sleep of right.

I awoke with the sound of the alarm clock and am raised to me more excited than usually. I got dressed, I had the breakfast that Graca, our employee, had already prepared, then I went to the university. I would have run with Kyle only in second period, but I did not need to go to his course to see it ravelling with a group of women fixed on his neck again. It stopped to discuss again with some of them, it seems that it is a routine for him. I continued to walk, and I exceeded it without me to trouble some, but the unexpected one occurred.

Kyle: Hello Miss Céline. I immediately stopped, turning the back to him, and it took me a few seconds to be turned over and look at it.

- I will know only that the day was good at the end.

Kyle: The girls, I will speak to you later, now I need to have a word with this pupil.

The girls dispersed whereas it went slowly towards me, deeply looking at me in the eyes, until it is with approximately eight inches of me.

Kyle: It is what your problem my daughter?

- My problem, it is you. I spoke with irony in exchange about his answer about the day before. This hidden smile reappeared.

Kyle: I must be a problem even Miss Celine, people tend to flee the problems because it is so difficult to leave there. Once the arrived problem, it left.

- I do not flee the problems professor. I am accustomed to destroying them. He closed the eyes and looked me of an aggravated air. Now, excuse me once again, I cannot be late for my course.

I turned the back again to him, but as it never stopped being satisfied, it stopped me again.

Kyle: Since how long do you make love with Miss Celine? I could not it believe when it asked me this question.

Who does he think of being? I thought. I turned to him perplexed.

- Which kind of question is this? You are insane?

Kyle: It is a question like another, you will not answer me?

- And what does that interest you, species of snooper? It still approached me and spoke again with my ear.

Kyle: Usually, if you are stressed like that, it is because you do not have sexual relationships.

You should kiss Miss Céline. I failed to fly on this blasted professor, but time ago, it moved away, leaving me planted in the middle of the corridor, and the worst, that even put to me late for the course. I went into blowing in my room, with fire in the eyes.

- Ah, small professor cretin, one does not lose to wait. I could not almost pay attention in class.

I felt my cheeks to burn with each time I remembered what he had said. I know that I am virgin, but that forever be a problem for me and that does not even have affected my mood. It is him which tracked me.

As of the end of the course, I left the red carpet my bag, I went to the door and I posed the carpet there. Everyone in the part looked at me, perhaps thinking of which point I am insane. One should not to him a long time to have arrived. It stopped just with the door, and fixed the carpet, and at the same time, it looked around the part in the search of me, and fixed its glance on me.

The part was quiet, and even the girls who dribbled in front of him did not have courage to accommodate it with the door. It took a few seconds, killing me out of the glance, then moved towards its office.

Kyle: Who put this carpet? All the room looked at me and I could not prevent me from laughing.

Kyle: What is there of so funny this time Miss Celine? Did you put the carpet over there? Of course, it knew that it was me, but as it wanted to exert its superiority, it did not let it pass unperceived.

- Did not love the professor? I propose to you to further go, since you are a prestigious and famous man among the female company.

Certain pupils started to laughing, the others also followed and laughed, and a few seconds later all the class laughed. I fixed the professor, pen in the mouth, waiting the moment when it would transfer me class. It moved towards my chair, under the glance curious about the pupils, and went back to speak to me with the ear.

Kyle: I adore the carpets Miss Celine, especially when I use them to kiss a woman. Did you know that the red color goes well to your skin? You would dissociate yourselves that one. Once more, I felt my cheeks to burn. It turned again me the back, went to its table and continued, this time while speaking so that all the class hears it.

Kyle: I adored the carpet Miss Celine, of all the women who offered it to me, you were most creative, then I see a way of rewarding the kindness.

- More than one son of... He made believe that I was another of these girls who continued to continue it, dying of desire of attention, beseeching a chance. I hate that. The buzz returned.

Kyle: Stop speaking the guy, pay attention classifies some now. He looked me with a smile snob on the face, and that gave me desire for making a murder with the intention to kill.

Chapter 4

The professor and the virgin nymphet mocker

I am not the kind of man who gives up himself with the women, I like to have capacity, to have control, this is why I am not accustomed to often maintaining me with the same person, therefore I do not run the risk to develop an emotional tie.

The majority of the women with whom I leave have my age or are older than me. It is not that I do not like to leave with young people, it is right which young people stick more quickly, and I do not want that a girl asks attention or for exclusiveness, but Céline woke up something in me that nobody waked up forever front, the desire for going to drive out, not because I want of it, but because I need some.

I must prove that it is as weak and easy as the others.

She gives me desire for defying it unceasingly, her glance is that of an wild animal and at the same time soft, its voice is soft and at the same time aggressive, it is one surprising mixture of girl and woman.

I returned at home by thinking of the way in which I should punish it for all aggressiveness with which it treated me and for all the comparisons that it made me.

- Old woman. If all the old men kissed like me, it would change opinion and would leave with them. I parked my car in my garage, and am dispatched to me to go to take a shower, because I was going to receive the visit of one of my pupils who repeated it in my article.

I knew that she wanted this course additional was only one excuse so that I kiss it, and it is not something which I do with no matter whom, but as it was one day enough stressing, I needed to discharge, therefore I would not deny it if she wanted. I took a shower, threaded comfortable clothing, but too relaxed, not put perfume and I was about to receive it when one sounded with the door.

Monique: Hello professor? She looked me from top to bottom, as usual.

I never slept with Monique, but it does not stop trying to arrange itself to leave with me and I always find an excuse, it is too sticking and I do not like that.

- Hello, you arrived just in time, you can enter. I spoke with sympathy. Monique: Does Kyle shit, this odor come from you?

- I think that yes, I answered. Which old song, I thought. I took it along in my study hall, it is a batch with books, tables and computers which I built myself.

I gathered all which I needed to help it, because even if I were ready to kiss it, it was to make a success of the test and I would do my work as I always did.

- You Sit, Monique. She looked me of a nostalgic air, but obeys. Monique: oh Ky, you know that I came here with other intentions isn't?

- Like that? I do not include myself/understand? I lied, I knew exactly what she wanted.

Monique: Do not try to play stray professor. He spoke, went back on his feet and approached me.

- Monique, you must have very an high note to make a success of my examination.

Monique: I know all your Ky businesses, that will go, I will not be made more bombard if you give me what I want.

- Then you took the express bomb? I already heard students speak about it, but I thought that it was really stupid for somebody of going badly on a chair, just to be able to kiss Prof I took all the comments like a joke, but now I see that it was true.

I have students psychopathes and stupid, because to harm their studies like that, it is very stupid.

- Then you will continue to make you evil if I do not give myself what you want? It approached even more, took off my shirt and sat me on the chair, and climbed on me, the isolated legs. Monique: It is not so hard Ky, do with me what you usually do with the others, you want?

She says by taking my hands and while placing them on her centres. I quickly felt my sex to take life.

Monique is a beautiful woman, but it is futile.

Monique: I feel already somebody to excite himself here. I put on her dress and I removed it. She carried a whole of black linen room, out of lace.

She took off my shirt and started to embrace my ear, making run her language in my neck.

- Stop. She looked at me surprised my refusal.

- Do you Know why I do not kiss anybody Monique?

Monique: Not, why?

- Because the majority want to order, try to exert a power on me, make insinuations, use their own body like soft food. I rose and I put it on his feet, in breeches and bra in front of me, and it did not include/ understand anything.

- If you want that I eat you, it will be my way, you include/ understand? It looked at me always frightened, but shook to it head in positive sign.

- Your bra Removes. It removed them, slowly. Its centres were small but hard.

- Now, remove your breeches. She obeys again, and removed her breeches, leaving it completely naked.

- Now, you sit on this table, while placing each foot on each side of this one, while opening to me

Completely. I say by indicating the square table out of wooden behind it.

And it is what it did, opening completely with me. It had the air obstructed a little by the exposure. I removed my currency and my boxer, putting to me entirely naked in front of it also. It devoured me eyes. My cock was hard and throbbing.

- Now, masturbates for me. It widened the eyes with my request, but slowly took one with its hands on its she-cat and started to be touched, and I made in the same way with a little distance.

Whereas it was touched and saw me touching me, it pushed small moanings and I saw his she-cat shining, showing at which point it was wet. Monique: Ky, I have am so excited to see you masturbating like that, please, eats me.

It was exactly the effect which I had on the women, the anxiety and the desire to be kissed by me. I approached it and I caught his two centres.

- I will tighten the nipples of your centres gradually, and you will say to me when you badly, included/understood? While waiting, continue to touch you. I started to tighten his nipples, and it closed the eyes, and I increased the pressure, and it started to groan and to shake more quickly, and I tightened a little more extremely, and it started to groan bruyamment and in an unverifiable way.

Monique: Oh Ky, I will come, continues to tighten, I go... Before it can finish its sentence, I left his centres and it opened the eyes seeking to know why.

Monique: Why didn't you continue? I was there almost. I turned the back without him to him to answer, I went in my room and I caught a condom. I returned, and it was in the same position, observing each one of my steps.

- Continue to touch you Monique. She started again to masturbate and I put the condom in front of her. I approached and I started again to tighten his nipples.

Monique: As it is nice this professor, so excited. When I realized that it was about to enjoy again, I said to him to stop shaking and I penetrated it, hard and violently.

I continued to tighten his nipple, more and more extremely, whereas she groaned like desperate.

Monique: Eat to me Ky, whore of good, oh as they is delicious. I felt his she-cat to tighten me, informing me that I was about to enjoy, then I gave up it.

- You will come only if I say that you will do it, you include/ understand?

Monique: She clearly excited and was blown.

- Now, you put at four legs on this table.

It was quickly rectified and was put at four legs, giving me a sight of initiate of its anus and its she-cat. I approached and I passed my language slightly on his anus, making him emit a small moaning, then I continued the Greek kiss with more intensity and she groaned more extremely. Monique: Whore of shit, which man it is, says it through her moanings. I used my fingers to masturbate it while I licked the bottom to him. Monique: Ky, I can about it more, I will come, I... I again gave up it, I removed it table and I took it along in my room.

- Goes up on my settee and continuous to four Monique legs. She obeyed, and I entered in her, I drew his long hair, I turned his hand and I started to penetrate it, more extremely than the first time.

I was extremely excited, dying of desire for enjoying, then I increased the speed of my movements by listening to Monique to beg itself to kiss it more extremely.

- It is really shitting. I thought I felt already his walls to be closed again.

- Taste quite hot, will taste. She was given to the orgasm, and I followed it, it was strong, intense and violent one, as I like.

I left my cock it, and it was on trembling legs, it sat down and looked at me.

Monique: Now I know why the women do not put themselves into four Ky, that is worth the blow to run to have a marvellous orgasm like that afterwards. If she thinks that I still will eat it, she is mistaken. I do not want a chewing-gum on my foot, thought I. Monique: I did not know that you liked this kind of sex of Prof.

- You do not know Monique large-thing, but now gets dressed, it is late, and I have appointments now.

Since you know already all the subject, I require a high note.

Monique: It is good Ky, I already had what I wanted, and you will have the acute note.

- It was right that which I needed, to exchange sex against a word which it needed.

It went to seek its clothing, got dressed and embraced me. Up to that point I had not had this contact with it, but the kiss was good, but nothing which can make me lose control.

I had still not found the good kiss. This kiss which makes me lose the notion of time and space. But if one day I find it, I could even think of the possibility of kissing the owner of this kiss more twice.

I thought. Monique left and I went to throw the condom and I took a long shower. My spirit brought me to Céline.

- Whore of nymphet misused. I spoke. I did not know why it had upset me as much. I needed to find a means of punishing it, I could not prevent me from thinking of it. I left to dine, benefitting from my own company, then I returned and I prepared to go to the bed.

Of course, I did not have any engagement, as I had said to Monique, I wanted just to quickly remove me from it. I lay on the bed and I ended up sleeping, without having the least idea than the following day this whore of nymphet was still going to make me shit.

I awoke, I took my coffee and I prepared to go to the university. As always, I arrived banished by students without one ounce of self-esteem.

I listened to them to chatter when I saw Celine passing, it was in the corridor not to only look at me then I decided to say hello. It stopped one moment and turned to me, giving me an answer badly high in front of the other pupils. I asked the others to leave, I walked towards Céline and asked him which was its problem.

PROFESSOR AND THE VIRGIN NYMPHET

She said that the problem it was me. I told him the same thing when she asked me the same thing the day before.

In addition to being shameless and mocker, it was also vindicatory.

When I said that I was really a problem, implying that she fled me, because she afraid to face me, she was said to me that she did not flee them because she was accustomed to destroying them.

She always had an answer specifies to give me, and that excited me. I looked it with challenge, but it was not long in saying that it was to go in class before I do not make it delay. When it turned me the back and moved away, I felt the need to face him more audacity.

I asked when was the last time that it had had sexual relationships. It stopped again and looked me with perplexity, not believing completely that I had courage to ask him that. In addition to me treating the insane one, it also treated me of snooper.

I approached it again, leaving our bodies very close one to the other and then I said to him to the ear usually that which does not have a sex saw stressed like it, then I said to him to have sexual relationships. I did not leave him time to answer, I was turned over while me ensuring that I had struck it in full face.

I again taught with the first class and I knew that the second class would be in its room, I were already prepared with his sour jokes, it with what I did not expect, it is that it would put a red carpet at the entry of the room. I was held in the embrasure of the door, trying to locate it, when I saw it, looking at me, while making fun. I climbed the carpet, walked to the table and requested which had posed the carpet on the door, even if I knew that it was it.

Even if I did not know it, the part delivered it of only one glance. She once again laughed, having fun with all the situation, and I asked him why she was so funny and if it were her which had put the carpet there, she confirmed it with largest grimace, and even said that was to honor the prestigious man that I am in the middle of the female company. It succeeded in making laugh all the room of the spectacle which it went up to expose me.

It looked me like an unpleasant girl, with a pen in the mouth, and that made me think of several things which I could make with this pen. I approached it and once again said to him to the ear that I adored the carpets and that I adored to use carpets for kissing women, and that its skin would arise on the carpet in question.

Then I am turned over to my office and I thanked it in front of all the room, by specifying that I would reward the gift. It was clearly obstructed, and I had enormously evil to thus see it. Once more, I sat down by making so that the table hiding place my cock.

The class whispered the ones with the others, and I asked for silence, trying to balance my thoughts, not to become insane just there with this whore of girl in the room, in front of everyone.

Chapter 5

The professor and the virgin nymphet perverse Professor

To kill professor Kyle after all that he said would not be an attitude as absurd, say as he asks it.

Whoever sees it teaching even thinks that he is a serious and exemplary pedagog.

- Which good example, a professor who lives by badgering his pupils, thought I.

I wanted to go to the toilets, I felt my breeches a little sticking, it was like that, after this cretin told me these unpleasant things.

I hate the fact that my body reacts to these things which it expresses. It would be really said that he wants to return me fascinated by him, and I refuse to fall into his dirty small chattering.

Kyle: I require that you answer this quiz immediately, his voice brought back for me to reality.

- Shit, I did not pay attention to all that he said. I thought. I looked at it and I was surprised to see it looking at me. It rose while the students were occupied answering the questionnaire and again moved towards the place where I was.

- Shit, I must stop sitting to me in front. I thought.

Kyle: I am sure that you did not pay attention so that I said.

- I keep silent myself, after all, it was right. Kyle: What is nine Misses Celine? Was so talkative, the cat ate your language? I am not kind to lower my guard with a male jerk, even less with this professor.

Does it have envies to play? I will learn how to you to play. I have looked around me, to see whether somebody analyzed us, when I saw that nobody looked at us, I looked at it and I put a smile on my face.

I beckoned to him to be squatted rather low so that I can say something to him to the ear. It made like me, looked around him, then leant, and I continued...

- My language has many uses, professor, contrary to yours, which is only used to say shit.

It looked at me seriously, not believing what I had just asked.

It scanned the part again, then brought a little its face closer to the mien. Kyle: My language has other uses which you do not know yet, but you soon will beg to meet Mr. Céline.

- Which ashamed son of whore. How could it make me wet thus? I met this cretin yesterday. I thought.

Kyle: There are wars, Miss Celine, that people are already ready to lose. It made the same smile narquois that the other times and left, turning over to its table.

So front, I doubted that he wants to convert me with his clan, now, I am sure. He knows me, I underwent several tests of fire not to lose my virginity with anyone, he could not nothing take to me, besides some spades which I will make in kind fall on him.

When its course was finally finished, a very pretty, but also very conspicuous woman approached her office and clears up the throat. It had the lowered head, reading a book, but then, it raised the eyes to look at it. Distance with which I was, I could not hear much things.

Not that I was interested by the contents of the conversation, but it seemed that they were very intimate one with the other. I rose to leave when it called me.

- That devil, this guy can only make fun of my face. I moved towards his table, where this woman looked at me head with the feet. I tried to be unaware of this futile glance of it.

- What you want Kyle. "Wow, which coarse way of speaking to the professor". Known as the woman by looking at me.

- Do Oh, you want that I speak to him as you do it? I can test, just a minute. I lowered the low neckline of my clothing a little, returning my centres very striking, then I made it tower of the table and I put my centres very close to his face, then I used the sexiest possible voice.

- Hello, beautiful mistress, that can I make for you, with share to lick the ground on which you steps? Can I give you a câlin? Wow, you feel so good. I involuntarily looked between his legs, and it was...

- Not, it is not possible, was excited it. How dépraver. I thought. It placed the book on its legs, to cover the major part of its pants.

I looked at the woman upright in front of us, who looked me with spite.

- What is nine meuf? Wasn't I rather good? I asked. "Girl, you are morveuse, you seem not to have still left the college, I am a woman."

- Oh, thank you very much, it is a compliment for me. Now, if you do not want to speak to me about anything about important, professor, I will go there, I must eat before the next course. I turned the back on both, but before it stops me.

- Wait, Mister. Celine. Monique, excuse us, I need to speak with Miss Céline alone. The woman did not seem much to appreciate it to have said to him to leave. When it left, I realized that there were only him and me in the class.

- I do not see myself taking some to you with another pupil that me, it is persecution. It rose of its chair, has makes it tower of the table and moved towards me, it was always held right. He noticed that I looked at his pants.

Kyle: Do you seek something, Mr. Céline?

- Yes, I seek your shame on your face.

Kyle: I guaranteed to you that you will not find it in my pants.

It approached a little more ego, making me shiver.

- Say to me what you want Kyle. It took to me by the size and pressed me on its desk.

- What do you believe that you make perverse? It stuck its body to the mien, making me dominate all its erection and I could not have any reaction, I just remained there, feeling my breeches to soak. Its eyes effleurèrent my centres and it made run one with its hands along my thighs. Kyle: Mr. Céline, I have the goose flesh on your skin, and I am sure that your breeches super are wet.

It raised a little the hand while I tried to control my breathing. I pushed it in an attempt at escape, but it caught up with me again and pushed me towards the table in the part. Kyle: Aren't you that which said to me that you were accustomed to crushing the problems, Mr. Céline?

You remove from this problem now. It used again its hand and climbed the interior of my thigh, approaching very close to my vagina.

- It is harassing Kyle, you will have troubles.

Kyle: Will you denounce me? Then, I would make better benefit from it to do what I want with you, since I will have troubles in any event.

- Despair started to invade me, I was virgin, and I never played this part to let myself touch so closely by somebody, even if I felt my vagina to cry for this touch.

- Kyle Shit, lets leave to me from here, say I with anger.

Kyle: What Mr. Céline, do you lose control? It did not stop moving its from top to bottom hand on my skin, trying to reinforce my anticipation. When it decided to climb a little more, concerning almost my breeches, the bell sounded, informing forthcoming course. I was relieved instantaneously.

Kyle: Saved by the gong. It let me leave, caught its business on the table, posed its bag in front of covering its erection and left, leaving me upright, completely excited, owe the part, incompetent to think correctly.

The students entered the room, and they did not include/ understand anything when they saw me like that. It is only whereas I felt the force in my legs to take some steps towards my chair.

I sat down by taking all the air in my lungs, in an attempt to calm me, because I was furious, makes the fury of it was not still sufficient to define what I felt.

- As you are stupid Celine. You could not show your excitation, now, it must think that it can lay down you like no matter whom of other. Oh, I hate that. I thought, but makes some, which I really wanted, it was to shout. I had to alleviate all my embarrassment and to concentrate me on the course before falling sick.

- Perverse Dumb. I blew, knowing that its perversion returned to me absurdly wet.

Chapter 6

The professor and the virgin nymphet To save by the gong

I made a smile narquois in Céline, so that it can see which was the owner, and it looked at me as if it wanted to strangle me.

I knew that my insinuation that she wanted my attention through the part would put it badly at ease.

Table is become my hiding-place personal, although my sex showed at which Céline point attracted me, I used my face to show the opposite, I do not want to let to him believe that it has any to be able on me. It had the air aired a little, then after him to have made think of the utility of the carpet for me, I could kiss it on the spot. She did not listen to exactly what I said.

I asked to the pupils to fill out a questionnaire, and I paid attention to the gestures of Celine, who obviously was surprised when it realized that I looked at it.

I was not going to miss the occasion to confront it, then I approached it and showed it not to pay attention in my class, which gave me reasons to think that it thought of all that I said to him.

It was quiet, which was unusual for it.

- What is nine Mr. Céline, were you so talkative, the cat ate you the language? I knew already at which point this girl was able to answer me all that she wanted, because I could already say that she was not the kind of girl who brings back shit to the house, but I did not expect that she uses my own methods to strike me.

It looked around it taking some great care not to draw the attention of the others and known as that its language was intact, because there are things which it can make only with it, as if that were not enough, it says that its language was several competent, contrary to the mienne which was used to say shit.

- Oh my beautiful, if you knew the capacity of my language, you would fall to four legs for me, thought I.

When I said to him that my language had capacities which she does not know, but that she would like to know, she was deafened, at the same time, I reduced it from her pedestal.

And I even said that there are wars in which people enter already to lose them. I had to turn the back again to him, because there is no woman in the world which never made me bandage as much as this nymphet made me.

I went to read a book while trying to change me the ideas on what the language of this girl could do with my cock.

The course was almost finished, and I could not walk also extremely in the corridors. When the course finished, Monique came to speak to me, I made fun at the same time, I already expected that it comes to seek me after to have eaten it the day before, but it was not with that I thought, whereas to some extent helped to control my erection. I did not pay attention so that she said, I have right fact attention in Céline who rose already to leave.

- Mr. Céline, can you come here please? I noticed that Monique looked it with attention, probably that it felt threatened by the incomparable beauty of Celine.

Of all my life, I never saw a girl more beautiful and sexier than Céline, but I will never say that to him, I am not insane to lose the capacity which I can have on it, even if it fights to hide it. Once again, she spoke to me with arrogance, seemed to be in anger, her impoliteness did not pass unperceived at Monique who started to thunder it. Celine used all her vice to face Monique, imitating the way in which it treated me.

The problem was when Céline left her deeper low neckline and brought closer her centres to my face.

- Whore, I will explode here. It was impossible not to bandage again, she had the capacity to make me bandage, even in moments simulated like this one. Celine noticed it, but Monique not.

I took the book and I put it on my legs to hide my cock. Monique and Céline disputed, which I knew would not carry out nowhere, Céline lost patience and left, but I had to ask Monique to leave, so that I can be alone with Céline. In spite of it, Monique withdraws herself.

I knew that at one time or with another, Céline would thunder me of me to take some with it, but it is exactly what I wanted that it realizes.

I put a point of honor to be approached it with a quite hard cock. It looked at my erection and I laughed internally to see it reddening.

When I asked what she sought in my pants, she said that it was my shame on my face. I confronted it and said to him that it was not my pants which it would find. It was enough that she asks me what I wanted, which I show him the lascif desire which exists in me.

I placed it against my office and made him feel at which point I was hard. She treated me of pervert, which returned to me even more excited. I looked at his low neckline and I wanted to remove his clothing to him and to bite the centres until to him she shouts while asking me to stop. She does not have any idea at which point I want to see it shouting on my cock.

I made run my hand on his thigh and I felt it to shiver. I have right makes him feel my fingers on his skin. I said to him that I knew that it was wet, and I tried to move my fingers a little higher, which made it try to flee.

I took it and took it along against the wall in which the table is, she would not escape to me so easily. I pointed out to him what she had said to me earlier, that she was accustomed to destroy the problems, then let it get rid of me.

I moved my hand towards the interior of his thigh, making it breathe a little more extremely. I did not take it with the serious one when she showed me harassing, she wanted to be touched, she was excited and would adore that I kiss it in the part, I could do what I wanted, I even had the idea, since I would have evil in any event.

I knew that it bluffait. It started to become nervous and practically begged me to release it, which even more justified me to continue. I asked whether it lost control, even if I knew the answer.

I raised my hand a little higher, and it was clearly nervous and excited, and at the time when I was on the point of touching his she-cat, our time was past. It pushed a sigh of relief, while I was frustrated not to have touched it in time. The body of Celine was like something of addictif, more I touched it, more I wanted to continue.

- To record by the gong. I spoke. I slackened it, I caught my bag and I left the part by hiding my cock which was absurdly hard.

My testicles hurt me and I needed really to empty them. I went to the toilets of the professors, I looked at if there were somebody, I locked the principal door, I went in the reserved part, I removed my pants and I started to masturbate me.

I did not stop imagining the small body carved of Celine on me, overlapping it and asking me to kiss it, this soft and soft voice, groaning whereas I entered and left it.

- Whore of shit Celine. I say while letting run all my liquid, imagining his small mouth licking all. I opened the shower and I washed myself, then I used a paper napkin to dry itself, I got dressed and I opened the door. I had chance that nobody wants to enter the bathroom while I struck one of them.

I went to have a coffee, because I had 40 minutes of free until the next course. I did not stop thinking that in every year of my professional life, I had never left with such a young girl, I saw on the disc which it had only 18 years, all in it was drawn perfectly, its mouth, its eyes, the freckles on it the skin, the stiff and russet-red hair, the centres in right measurement, the bottom then? I am not either able to speak without becoming again hard. I never thought of a woman with whom I kissed to masturbate,

when I struck one of them, I always had resort to pornographic vidéos, but to strike Céline, even if I never kissed it, was something which worried me. It was enough that this girl makes fun of me, that I think that I was to have it.

- Shit, which ended up being made foutre, it is me. I spoke. I need to eat this nymphet, I do not know how I will have it, but it will climb on my cock.

Chapter 7

The professor and the virgin nymphet To think of him

To sit down on the chair with wet breeches and to always try to pay attention in class were a true test of fire.

All my being was on fire and that returned to me extremely in anger. I refuse that this professor treats me like one unbalanced, and I as refuse to show him as it succeeded in one way or another interesting me in another thing that his class.

In fact I in war with him, I were in war with myself, was I in a fight between the reason and the emotion was not, or should I say the desire? I never liked to think that the sex can be done without feelings, I believe that you must have feelings so that the sex occurs.

I do not admire particularly those which manage to separate the two things, because it is as if the body were an object which can be used by no matter whom, shameless nor concern, and people who treat the sex so liberally make me think of which point they are empty are.

I do not need to know professor Kyle to know which kind of swindler it is. You can see it in the way in which it treats the women, trying to pay attention to everyone with an aim of having always an open door to take them along to the bed. They do not even realize that it makes a mental selection to decide which is worth or is not worth the sorrow to be eaten.

If they knew that men as that is not worth the ground on which they go, they would develop their body better and would not offer them to this jerk so that it does what it wants.

And it is by thinking like that, that I prevented some from benefitting from me. I know exactly at which point I am beautiful, and at which point my standard of beauty is rare, and I had to learn how to defend me, and my strategies functioned for a long time, until this cretin appears in front of me to claim my attention.

The course finished, and once again I did not pay attention to it, nor to both others after it.

I remained in the living room all the time, even if I needed to go to the toilets, avoiding the risk crossing Kyle in the corridors.

At the end of the courses, I went to my car to haste, despaired to return to the house and to extinguish fire between my legs. As soon as I returned, I went directly in my room and did not even answer Graca when she asked to me whether I wanted to lunch. I was hungry, I had not eaten anything between the courses, but I had need of time far from the glances, I needed intimacy. I locked the door of the room, I removed my clothing and I had only my breeches, which were still wet. I went in front of the mirror and I looked at my body.

I slipped my hands on my centres and tightened them, imagining that they was the hands of the professor. Then I passed a hand on my legs and remembered his touch, which was so light but left a whole way of desire. I recalled all the way which he had traversed and I closed the eyes, remembering its erection between my legs.

- Oh professor, I in the middle of the moanings say. I went to my breeches, which were again soaked, and I slipped my hand inside, while the other was pressed against my chest.

I reopened the eyes and I started to masturbate me by looking me in the mirror, so abandoned with the desire and excited.

I imagined that it was him which touched me, tightened me and desire made me sigh. I brought closer my legs to try to feel to touch it more firmly and I increased the speed of my hand on my clitoris.

Whereas I moved my hand, I let escape from small moanings. I felt that I was going to enjoy, and I closed the eyes, giving up me with the pleasure.

- Kyle... I called it, as if each part of my body answered him.

- It will be a secrecy between us, say I by looking at my reflection. I would never admit that I masturbated while thinking of him.

And I would do anything so that it does not touch me any more.

I needed to center me on my studies, and this burning desire that I feel for this man can wound me.

My parents involve me to excel in all that I undertake. They justify me to seek to be the best in all than I undertake. Thus I cannot drop them while packing me with things like that.

- It was right a masturbation, that will not go beyond. I spoke. I prepared the bath-tub and I went to take a shower, and that did not disturb me to spend as much time under water. My body needed to slacken. I was tended by all that had occurred in two thin days from school. It is absurd which the things change so quickly. As soon as I left the bathroom and that I went in the room, Graca struck with my door.

Graca: Celine, your friend is there. I did not even need to ask which friend, I have only one of them.

- Ask him to come please. I unbolted the door and it entered like insane.

It always does that, to enter and throw themselves on my bed.

- Sometimes I think that you are 60 years old Karen. He lives while playing everywhere where he feels at ease.

Karen: It is because I am tired, but I do not manage to leave this double life.

- I do not know how you make to work with the woman of your customer, as so of nothing was not.

Karen: When I accepted this work, I did not know that her husband was right the guy who kisses me.

- But you could have stopped leaving with him.

Karen: Be insane for you? The guy spoils me, I will not lose my advantages simply because I work with his wife.

- You are terrible.

Karen: I became a little colder and more computer after you to have met.

- Is Oh, maintaining it of my fault? I say while laughing.

Karen: Perhaps.

- Oh, does not lower your dog.

Karen: Now I must return at home, because this evening I will serve a very hot customer and it is one of the customers best paid, the weekend I do not want excuses, one leaves to give pleasure.

- As long as you do not have a male while you are with me, that suits me, I am not mood to be held of the candles.

Karen: You should authorize to you to also take a male, to stop being virgin and to discover as they is good to eat.

- I did not spend as much time to flee a male asshole, to give to whoever one night of festival.

It rose and went to the door, but initially that disturbed me a little more.

Karen: If you continuous like that, you will die with your covered she-cat, creating a cobweb.

I caught a sandal and I launched it towards it, but it closed the door in time to avoid being touched.

Karen was my friend, I do not say who it is the best because I have only it, but if I had some another, Karen would be definitively the best.

It is 23 years old and is graduate in physical education, it teaches part-time in a gymnasium and is an escort of luxury.

It leaves with a guy for nine months who gives him all, he even paid its silicone, and after having started to work with the gymnasium, she discovered that the husband of the owner was the same guy, i.e. both paid its wages.

She was surprised but continued to leave with him. I already said that one hour the house crumbles. It did not seem to be concerned with it. She wants just to save money and to make the round the world tour. Let us say that she works to pay

the expensive voyages which she wants to make, even if she made already much, because much of these guy take along it in the voyages which they make without their family.

The men all are similar, it is enough to change address. I know that it is a little contradictory that I would be if reserved and that I have a friend like that, so much as the women whom I do not stop criticizing, but I did not know that it was as that when I started to like it.

Now, I live in this abusive relation, loving a whore completely different from me. I am the only one with being able to treat it of whore, nobody other.

Joke with share, it is a good friend, it can be and do what it wants of her life, but it forever dropped me as a friend, it leaves any customer in plan if I need it.

The only problem, it is that it does not stop saying to me to lose my virginity so that I know what is well. I do not need any man to satisfy me.

After me to be repaired, I am descended to eat, because I could not retain my hunger any more.

- Grace, I am hungry.

Graca: He is Céline a little late, you want to lunch or lunch?

- To lunch, I would make better eat well. It heated my food and I ate while thinking of my life which was already very wild. It is incredible as a thing can influence all the remainder. After having eaten, I am turned over in my room and I went to study. I needed to recover the contents which I had lost.

I hid my face in the books, and when I finished, the weather was already black. I was surprised that my parents did not return yet of work. They worked together in a law firm. Graca: Celine, the dinner is ready and I am on the way. Your parents called and said that they were going to be late a little and that you could dine without them.

- Of Graca agreement, thank you. I was useful myself and I dined, feeling me only, I started to be depressed while thinking of which point my life was stopped and without emotion.

I am 18 years old and I do not know how to live like people of my age. Perhaps that I could be a little less authoritative with myself.

SOPHIA

After the dinner, I am turned over in my room and I lay on the bed, when my cellphone sounded. I rose and I still took it inside the bag, and I saw that I did not know the number.

- Hello? Nobody answered me, I just heard somebody breathe bruyamment with the other end of the wire.

- Hello? What is this? The person remained quiet.

- If you do not say anything, I from go away. "Mr Céline". I was without voice when I heard the thick voice with the other end of the wire. How did it obtain my number? Whore, of course that it had my number, it was my professor.

- I hope that you invited me to speak about something related to your matter professor.

Kyle: In fact, I invited to know how was your breeches, Miss Céline.

More than one shameless son of whore. I thought.

- Professor, you do not have the capacity to leave my breeches in precarious situations.

Kyle: Mr. Céline, I am sure that you wet yourself just because of my touch. You do not have the capacity to control your libido when you are close to me.

- Would not be idiotic Kyle, you are not enough man to make me sigh, without speaking about my libido.

Kyle: It will be seen whether you are right really ms. Celine. Tomorrow is a new day, good night. I remained the opened mouth, without saying a mot. It hung up again and I was still deafened.

- This man can follow only one course with the devil. Which cretin. It was not enough that it made of my day a hell, now it will make my thoughts a hell the night.

I felt a light tingling in my vagina, but this time I would be strong.

Chapter 8

The professor and the virgin nymphet To think of her

I like the sex, I like to have capacity, I like to see a subjected woman, I like to tighten, bite and to whip, I like to look at them tasting my cock and I like to push their head towards the stem.

I like the feeling which I have begging me when I hear them groan, to push more extremely.

I like to suck their she-cat until they twist of everywhere, then to put my cock in them without their leaving time to breathe. I am not always an animal with the bed, because everyone does not like this style of sex, but when I find somebody ready to deliver this way with me, I pass on another mode. I do not know how I will react if I were likely to kiss Céline.

What that would make if I put my cock in his delicious mouth, or what that would make press its nipples.

I become excited by imagining it very naked and smiling in front of me. My hand would be marked perfectly on this hot bottom that it A.

- Whore of shit. I am become again hard and there remain only 5 minutes before I turn over in class.

I thought. Fortunately that there was nobody around me. I concentrated on the reading of a book while my cock started again to behave.

I turned over in class, and gave the two latest quotations of the day. I remained to go to lunch with Eduardo, an old friend of festival. I returned at home, I took a shower and put more relaxed clothing, then I went to meet it.

- This animal never ages, say I as soon as I arrived at the table where it was already.

Eduardo: My wife has sports a hall, my son, it does not stop being caught some with me so that all is in order, but you are not badly either, you must eat much women to remain like that.

- Some yes, all within the established limits. I sat down and we caught up with all the conversation.

Eduardo is 32 years old and has a multinational, and with the precipitation of its work and of the mien, it was a little difficult to us to plan a date, but it is like me, although he is married, he saw while jumping over the fence and by taking a woman hotter than the other, the only difference is that he tends to stick to it.

- Then is Edu, which woman this time? Eduardo: Ky, I am with blonde a 23 year old, large, sexy and a delight with the bed, but...

- Shit, it must have one there but.

Eduardo: It is an escort of luxury, I paid it once and now, I want to always pay.

- Without Edu joke, therefore a food granfino?

Eduardo: But it is signal Ky, it makes a delicious pipe, in addition to being beautiful, it is a whore of woman.

- And you see it since when?

Eduardo: That made nine months.

- Last nine months ? Are guy, you insane? This woman will tear off you the heart if you remain with it.

Eduardo: Worse than I am in love with this bitch of Ky, and the worst, I will not even say myself it.

- I am even afraid to ask.

Eduardo: Did my wife engage a new physical teacher for the gymnasium, and guess which it is?

- Es you serious whore? You can only joke with Edu. Does your lover work in the sports hall of your wife?

Guy, that will be really bad. It is obvious that will not function Edu. Eduardo: The worst, it is of having to control me when I arrive at the sports hall and that I see it, with this behavior.

- You do not have really any direction, say I while laughing and it followed.

Eduardo: And you do guy, you always want anything serious with nobody?

- My business is right of kissing and to pass to the following, I do not want that somebody sucks me energy, but a new coed arrived at the university, young person, it is 18 years old, which returns to me insane, guy.

Eduardo: What is it? Then you which lose the head for nothing nor nobody, you crack for an young girl?

- In fact, she does not even speak Edu to me, she is absurdly impertinent, ironic, arrogant, she is not afraid to say what she thinks, and she continues to face to me in front of all the room.

The girl is a plague, in addition to being beautiful, russet-red, all well done, the vision of the sky, but it does not run me literally afterwards like the others.

Eduardo: Oh, I include/understand. What held your attention, it is the fact that she does not want to suck you like the others. He says while laughing.

- Let us say that it has an high degree of difficulty. So that I reach it, I will have to better do my, I feel put at the challenge to obtain it.

Eduardo: And if you succeeded and that you end up falling in love?

- You remove me Edu? When did you see me in love? The intention is to make it fall in love with me, and I can eat it when I want. It is losing. Eduardo: Pay attention not to lose and forget the way of the return, guy. He says while laughing once more. We spent the hours to speak, and we reserved an exit for the weekend, it will not travel, therefore it will be free to benefit from the night. And another that the life is not only work. When I returned at home, it made already night, I went to take a shower, then I went to separate the material for the course which I was going to give the following day.

When I thought of run, it was impossible not to think of Céline.

- Will Whore, it be always like that now? Will I think of this girl all the time? I wondered, but knowing the answer already.

I could not any more prevent me from thinking of it. I lit my laptop and I sought files containing of the data on the students, such as the complete name and the telephone, and I sought to it his.

- It is here, Miss Céline. I took my cellphone and I composed his number, little time after she answered. I remained quiet, listening to his soft voice. She asked which it was, and I remained quiet. When she threatened to hang up again, I answered.

- Mr. Céline. She remained quiet one moment and I wondered how she reacted to my voice. Then, she said that she expected that I invite it to speak about my history. She knew badly that I invited just to hear his voice, but I was not going to reveal it. I thus put questions about his situation of breeches, which annoyed certainly it.

She said that I did not have the capacity to leave his breeches in precarious situations, and I rétorqué that it was her which did not have the capacity to control her libido when she was close to me. She said that I could not make it leave sighs, without speaking about her libido. I left a promise which we would see whether it were really true. I made an indirect threat, and I was sure to give him one night filled of conjectures and anguishes.

- Ah Mr. Céline. Shit, it was the moment when you decided that you had to be able more that me.

Chapter 9

The professor and the virgin nymphet the capacity is with me

Taking into account my antecedents missed with the men, I was ready with me to take some to the professor if I continued to allow him to enter my spirit.

I rose early, ready to make his day a hell. If he likes to embarrass me at the university, which is a place of studies, I would make him taste the same poison.

I opened my wall cupboard, and I chose a black dress, which was extremely close to my body, and which left half of my exposed thighs, with a low neckline very striking, and a zipper on the bust which enables me to increase the size of the low neckline if I wanted. I took a shower, washed my hair, hydrated my skin, then dried my hair which was perfectly smooth then I am equipped, and I chose not to carry breeches not to mark the dress.

I put a lipstick Bordeaux wine and the perfume expensive which I had. I put high sandals, I took my material of study and I went to the university. As of my arrival at the university, I saw by far the same depressing scene like always.

- It is if this guy does not weary himself to be a womanizer like that? I say myself by approaching me the professor and his band of fanatics of the sex. I walked of a firm step and I increased my step, I kept the head high and the right back and I drew the attention of everyone with each step which I took. "This small nice thing". "Which scented cat". "Come always here, my darling"? "Me your delicious number Gives". It was a joke after the other which I was to hear. If there is a thing which I know, it is which the man is attracted by what it sees, then I would show with this small professor what it is to have of the capacity.

As soon as I approached it, the girls started to look me with desire.

I know this glance with kilometers.

The professor looked at behind, and I ensured myself to fix it at each step which I took, then I diverted the glance, and I am sure that made it insane.

I would not have run with him, but that would not prevent me from putting my action plan. It did not call me like the preceding time, and I expected it, it had to feel my intention at the time when I looked at it, and saw that it was to better keep its distances. There remained still 15 minutes before the beginning of the course, I left my bag in the room and I went to the wall where there were all the schedules of all the rooms and I sought in which room Kyle would teach.

I went to seek the room and I quickly found it, it had already sat at his office, speaking with a blonde, who dredged it obviously. I entered the part and I tried to be unaware of the whistle of the jerks in the part. When the professor saw me, it quickly changed its posture, which was slackened before, then tended. I arrived at table, I looked at the peroxide blond in front of me and I tried to be as friendly as possible.

- Hello Madam, sorry to stop your conversation with the professor, but I about an private affair, then can you would like to speak to him excuse us? I promise to be fast.

The blonde looked me with mistrust, perhaps was it curious to know of what it acted, but she smiled as wrongfully as she did it then left. I placed the two hands on the table, and looked at the fair one moving away, then fixed the professor, who always hid the same half smile.

- Do you Find what I did funny professor? I approached him, taking a book of constitutional law which was on the table, I opened a page, and made pretense raise a question not to wake up the suspicions of the students.

I leant so that my centres are very close to its face.

- Then Professor Kyle, at the time of your call of yesterday, I noticed that you like to speak about breeches.

Kyle: Not always, I like to speak only when they are wet, which will be the case of yours in little time if you continue to try to tease me Mr. Céline.

- Afflicted professor... I made a pause and I spoke with his ear... It is right which today I do not have of breeches,

Thus you will not be able to wet them. I ensure you that I do it, I will leave this cock throbbing while thinking of my she-cat all the day with overdraft. Even in this moment, you must think of which point it must be easy to penetrate. I looked at it and addressed a malicious smile to him by seeing it closing its hand on the table.

Ah, poor professor Kyle, it must be very badly at ease over there. I say by looking at his erection, which jumped obviously out of its pants.

Kyle: Mr. Céline, I charge generally much with those which measure usually the forces with me.

- We are thus two professors, you will have to work hard to obtain what you want so much.

My she-cat is not for the male which walks while putting the roller in each she-cat that he sees in front of him.

You will want perhaps even to make me pay expensive, but I pay only if I want it. I closed the book, turned the back to him and directed me towards the door, accompanied by other whistles. I went in my room with a victorious smile on my face, of course I were not going to give him my she-cat but it will be amusing to make him believe that it can have it if it learns how to behave.

- Glad to have succeeded in paying attention in progress this time, I say myself as of the end of the course. I rose and I went to the toilets before the beginning of the second course.

When I entered, the girls left, leaving the empty bathroom, which I adored, because I had thus more intimacy. I entered the cabin and I made wee, and I used shower head to wash itself, because I hated that my she-cat feels the urine, then I dried myself with a paper napkin.

I noticed that somebody had entered the bathroom and had heard the noise of the key which one closed. I was already in alarm because the principal door must always be open not to disturb the entry of those which want to use the bathroom.

I opened the door and I went to see who it was, and at the same time I was pushed back in the cabin.

- What do you believe to make? I shouted as soon as I realized that it was Kyle. It posed its hand on my mouth, preventing me from speaking.

Kyle: Calm Mrs. Celine, I came to show you what arrives to the girls who try to measure the forces with me. The stand is tiny, and the fact that it is small me kept, me and the professor, very close relations one of the other.

I tried to leave, but its body wedged the door. It withdrew its hand of my mouth, and I did not shout, and it knew that I would not do it. We were in duel and none us wanted to lose. Both wanted the capacity of the situation.

- Lets leave Kyle to me, I will miss my run.

Kyle: There remain still 10 minutes, and I promise that it will be sufficient.

- Enough for what?

Kyle: To make you cry Miss Céline. It drew the zipper from my dress in extreme cases, leaving my two exposed centres, I tried to hide them, but it removed the tie around my neck, took my two hands and held them.

- Lets leave Kyle now to me. I spoke by tightening the teeth. He was unaware of me and placed my hand tieds above my head, and held me with a hand, preventing me from moving, while the other went up my legs to my she-cat which was already soaked by its touch.

- For the moment with this Kyle, I say by feeling despair to invade me.

I was afraid that it penetrates me and discovers that I am virgin. It continued to be unaware of me and passed its fingers on my she-cat.

Kyle: Where is Mr. Céline your capacity now? He looked me in the eyes, whereas he started to shake me, I tried to release taken once more, and he tightened me more and more extremely.

He caught my centres, and bit making their nipples, me push moanings that up to that point I tried to retain at all costs.

He pressed on my clitoris, and increased the movements and I closed the eyes, completely overcome, feeling the orgasm to arrive with all and to consume me the heart. Until without any scruple, I groaned, releasing all my pleasure in its fingers.

Kyle: Learn something, Mr. Céline. Even if you do not want to pay me, I obtain my payment.

It released my hands, slipped its tie into its pocket, then opened the door and left. I intended the door to be unbolted whereas I tried to find the movement of my legs.

- Shit, shit, shit.

Which wire bastard of whore. How does it make to have such a domination on me? Oh which hatred. I say by closing again my dress, ghost to wash my sticking she-cat.

I dried myself then directed me towards the mirror, trying to organize my dress. I had to wet my face to recover. Then I went in class and I was constrained to be late. I was concentrated so much on the fingers of the professor on my she-cat which I did not even hear the sound to turn over in class. I passed the remainder of the morning to feel my skin to crawl only by remembering that it had touched me, and my she-cat was again wet.

I thanked it mentally when it vwas finally time to leave. I precipitated towards my car, I removed my sandals and I tried to return at home as quickly as possible. I wanted to take a shower to extinguish the fire which consumed to me without requiring the permission.

I entered the house and I once again was unaware of Graca, it must think that after having begun the university, I became insane. I went in my room, I locked the door, I stripped myself and I went under the shower.

- Which hatred, I shouted while remembering him sucking me the centres, and I refused to again touch me while thinking of him. It could not have ego as much, whereas it gave me only the residue of what it remained of him, which lives by kissing other women. I could not lend to me to this role, it would be necessary that I would be stronger than that if I want only to have one chance to gain it.

Chapter 10

The professor and the virgin nymphet Fetishes

I cannot give up so that Céline devotes itself to me, I do not support to see it looking me with indifference, as if I were any man, I am not no matter who, and I am far from the being.

I awoke with a hard cock, and before going to the university, I went to the toilets to strike one of them, while thinking of it, and with the despair which it felt when I pressed it with the council of the university.

To think of it as that so often became dangerous, because I do not need to be wedged with a 18 years nymphet which still does not know what is to only be really happy.

- It had to sleep with a band of inexperienced boys who do not know how to make enjoy a woman in a masterly way.

- Today, I will not learn to him, which will not leave me space to touch it again. So only it knew at which point I want it. I say by threading my tie.

I arrived at the University and I prepared with daily harassing. There were too many centres, bottoms and she-cats to be managed, but none them was Céline.

- That becomes a little obsessional, thought I. I did not pay really attention so that these women said, but I paid attention when they ceased speaking and looked at all unit a specific corner behind me. When I looked at behind, I was immediately transported in hell.

I say the hell, because my body started to heat way absurdity, and the air started to miss, with each step which it took. It was not other than Miss Celine, vêtue of an extremely sexy and daring dress which left its perfectly formed curves and its visually projecting centres.

- Shit, which infernal girl. I thought. She fixed me, and I was lost in his glance, which showed at which point she was malicious, diabolic and stupidly shameless.

When it diverted the eyes, I felt given up and at the same time tried to claim his attention again, would be this only for one half-second. I gave up when I realized that I was hard, and without my handbag, it would be impossible to hide my erection. Same manner that the women dribbled on me, the guys dribbled on it, and I felt anger to invade me, or can I say that it was jealousy?

- Not, it is impossible for me to feel me jealous of a nymphet deceived like that in if little time.

Not after it snobé me and confronted me. I refuse to feel anything for this girl.

I left the women who accompanied me and directed me towards the room where I was going to teach. I would like to be able to sit me and breathe, to take again the control of my body. As soon as I finally arrived at my table,

Rebecca approached. It was a coed who redoubled also my course, and it tried me at all costs to make it eat in exchange of an high note to the test which I pass in a few days. Rebecca: Professor, whom do I have to make so that you give me an high note with this test? he with a smile narquois asked.

- You must initially study Rebecca. I say while turning over the smile.

Rebecca: There is not a simpler means? I did not even answer, I were completely tended when I saw this demon invading my room.

- Didn't Whore of shit, I even have time to recover well, what it wants with that? Returns to me insane?

I thought. The worst, it is to listen to these guys to dredge it, as if it were so easy to draw its attention.

PROFESSOR AND THE VIRGIN NYMPHET

It arrived at my table, asking Rebecca to leave us quiet, using a sympathy which I knew that it did not have, after all, the girl had an high level of vice and claim.

Knowing Rebecca like me, it left only because Céline used this false sympathy, and I paid attention to his excellent performance and it was impossible not to laugh at the situation. It posed its hands on my desk, and disfigured me, and when it realized that I appreciated his attitude, it took my book, opened it on a page and approached me, and made pretense speak about the mienne, leaving its centres almost rubbing my face, I knew that it acted like that purposely, I tried to control my extinction, not to bandage again.

It was shown more daring than ever, and questioned me on my taste to speak about breeches, which were the subject of the call that I had passed the day before to him. I included/understood exactly what it tried to do, and I felt confronted with his audacity, and I said to him that I liked to speak only about wet breeches, and I threatened it that his would resemble that if it continued to try to tease me.

- Which whore of dumb. She succeeded in breaking my control once and for all, making my cock hard like stone. She saw my situation, and yet she was not satisfied.

She began with me snober, saying that she was to be badly at ease in my pants, and she was it really.

I had the impression that somebody tightened me the testicles and my cock really palpitated. She knew that I did not have any capacity over there, in front of my pupils, and she used it with her advantage.

I threatened it again, and said to him that I was accustomed to dearly charging those which tried to measure the forces with me; but it did not move back, on the contrary.

She was more than clear that she was not satisfied with my sexual distractions and that I could not eat it if I did not give up my sexual activities with other women. She wanted exclusiveness, and I would not give it to him, because I knew that she would not be so strong to resist my advances, and I would not have to stop kissing other girls, knowing that I can have it in any event.

She turned me the back and withdrew herself, showing her bottom flashy, and once more I was irritated against the guy who whistled towards her.

- You pay me your demon. I thought. The course started and I had need of time to calm me before raising me.

- This girl should not have done that during my time of class, I never let anything interfere with the quality of my courses, and it made me do it for the first time. I could not give a teaching of quality while thinking of his whore of she-cat. At the end of the course, I had to excuse me near the pupils not to have given them the complete material, but that I would give it to run according to.

- Fuck Celine, I will kill you. I thought. I benefitted from the pause which I always had from one course to another, and I went to see what it did, I would not teach the second period, but it would have course, and I needed to benefit from this pause.

While arriving in the corridor, I live it by far to move towards the toilets of the women. I walked behind it, not letting it notice me, and looked at it entering the bathroom. I went in the bathroom of the men, who was right beside that of the women, that took a few minutes to me, and I decided to go in the bathroom of the women, I opened it a little before entering to see whether there were a girl inside with share she, and there was not, I entered quickly and locked the door, and looked under the cabins deprived to make sure that we were really alone.

Until it reaches the last and realizes that it was there that she was. I waited until it opens to be able to enter and to lock up it inside.

As soon as it opened it, I entered the cabin and it looked at me frightened, asking me aloud what I did. I posed my hand on his mouth, even if I knew that she would not shout. I said to him that I would show him what arrives at whoever tries to measure its force with me, and it tried to escape. I withdrew my hand of his mouth and she asked to leave not to be late in progress, but I said that we still had enough time and she asked why, and I said that I would make it cry.

I closed it too quickly so that it tries to stop me, and I left his delicious discovered centres, but it used its hands to cover them. I immediately removed my tie and attache his two hands, and it required that I release taken, but I did not do it. I held his hands above his head and I used my other hand to reach his she-cat which was very wet. It was clearly desperate and asked me to stop, but I did not have any intention to stop. I passed my fingers slightly on his she-cat and I asked where was its capacity, and it looked me without anything to say. I started to masturbate it, and it tried to release taken, but I am much stronger than it and I tightened it more extremely, I started to suck and to crush its centres, which were soft and pink, and it groaned while returning to me insane.

I could kiss it there, in all possible ways, and I could make it conceal with my cock in his small mouth, but it needed to understand that it would not be so easy to make me eat, I have my value, and it was not with the capacity, but me if.

I pressed on his clitoris and increased the movements, and I live it to close the eyes and to be given thoroughly with me, it groans délicieusement, giving me desire for eating it, but I could not, I needed to be strong.

They was delicious and exciting to see it thus delivered, and its breath made go up and to kill his centres and I imagined to tighten his nipples extremely, but it was still too early to make him discover the pleasure which exists in the pain.

It came on my fingers, and I saw the occasion dreamed there to give my failure chechmate. I looked at it, completely broken up, and I said that even if she did not want to pay me, I tore off my payment to him.

I released his hands, unbolted the door, even with my hard cock, and I left in the toilets the men.

I knew that the bell had already sounded, but I did not have run at this time. I locked the door of the bathroom of the men, as I did the other time in the bathroom of the professors, I went to empty my cock, which already badly made me have retained sperm during so a long time. I removed my pants and my underclothing, left my cock and am masturbated to me while thinking of its delicious, hard and pink centres.

- Lets puff out you to me Céline, ah, which delicious she-cat, which whore of exciting. Finally I came, leaving all my liquid on the wall of the bathroom.

- I become more perverse than front. I spoke by cleaning the wall. I cleaned, then equipped, feeling me much more relieved.

- This girl returns to me insane, completely vulnerable with the simple possibility of eating it. I left the bathroom and I went in the classroom to recover the bag which I had left on the table.

- Excuse to me Tavares, I just will seek my bag, say I while entering the part. As soon as I arrived at table, he whispered me with the ear.

Tavares: Were you already ready to become tall? Tavares was a pal of work which ate all the she-cats that he saw, he corresponded to the schedule of conditions of Celine, in addition to me accompanying at the time of the evenings that the students organized the weekend.

- How did you guess? I played. It lowered the eyes on my pants and I followed his glance.

Tavares: Do not forget to close the zipper the next time. I hid the zipper with my handbag and I left while laughing. Arrived outside the part, I closed again the zipper and directed me towards the office of the senior, who again ate the secretary on the table.

- Eder Shit, closes the door when you are active. I while turning the back to him and with Mrs. say. Paula who had half of her age. She got dressed quickly and left, without me to look with embarrassment.

I just shook the head and me sitted on the chair opposite him.

- Did you already imagine if it were your wife who entered here? Fact this business well Eder.

Eder: It never comes here and you are a jerk.

- I am content that it is me, I could have been student, and one would speak about you here. Eder: It which speak here Kyle, which does not see the tail of the skirt and wants to already put its hand inside, I know already the new student, you know that if you find yourself with the council for harassing, I will not have any means of defending you, isn't this is you?

- Relaxed Eder, that will not arrive. Eder: Made right attention when you enter by effraction the bathroom, someone else that me can see it. He spoke by showing the images on the computer, that the cameras took when I entered the bathroom. - This is why I came here. Erase that from there, and the images of the class when I put my hand in his she-cat.

Eder: The rules are clear Kyle, these images must spend one month here, until we are sure that nobody will denounce himself, because we need evidence if somebody would come here while saying that it was badgered by you and if the police force asks for these images, I will have to provide them. Although we know exactly what occurs here, this rule is the only one which cannot be modified. In 30 days, when it is sure, I will erase your spite.

- Of agreement, but that will not arrive. I say while raising me of the chair. When I arrived at the door, I looked at it and recalled him to close the door the next time. While passing in front of the secretary, I said to him hello, knowing that would still more badly put it at ease.

- I am terrible, I know. I do not give up having fun. The university is one of best of California, and it there forever have exactly anything which tarnished its name or that of the senior.

The reputation of the university is irreproachable, but nothing of what occurs in its walls is forced or not agreed, i.e. until Céline arrives and makes me make this madness.

What I did could really be regarded as harassing, but I just like knew at which point she wanted to be touched by me, I aspired to the day when I could put my cock in his she-cat. I gave the other courses of the day with more care, because I did not want to remake to fail my pupils. But I knew at which point my spirit fought not to think of the moanings of Celine whereas I shook it. There became increasingly difficult to remain concentrated on my work. At the end of my quarter of work, I stopped in a pharmacy to restock my stock of condoms, the employee, seeing the excessive quantity of packages, tried to hide his smile.

I pointed out pretense nothing, but I wondered already what passed to him by the head. To carry the reputation to be a womanizer was not at all awkward for me, after all I owed allegiance with nobody, and I could kiss morning, midday and evening, and nobody had nothing to do there. I returned at home, I removed my clothing and I went to take a shower. And the groaning voice of Celine continued to resound in my ears, and my cock became hard as with each time I am surprised to think of it. I needed to sleep with somebody since I could not sleep with Céline, but I did not want to call any of my contacts, then I had the brilliant idea to call an escort of luxury. I left the bathroom, I threaded clothing and I sought on Internet a reliable site which offered an high quality service to me.

I made contact and I said that I was interested only by the sex and that I would not leave nowhere. The agency sent a list of girls available to me and I threw a quiet glance with each one.

And that in question drew my attention. It had the clear skin, the black hair, the sculptural body and the charming smile, it was the type of woman whom I would eat easily.

I chose it and I already agreed on the value with the agency, I gave him the address and it arrived one hour later. Its nickname was Kaka, that could have been Kaka for Karine, Kate, for Karen, but that did not have any relevance, the important one was that I was going to kiss it.

- He good night. I say as soon as I opened the door to him.

Kaka: Good night cat. It entered and I saw the exubérance of his bottom, and its centres clearly made me understand that it was silicone, I prefer the natural ones, but it was only one detail.

- Good pussy, I too much will not fix then I go right to the goal. I know that you are paid by the agency, but I am ready to pay you the same one going up outside so that you make certain my requests.

Kaka: Am Oups, I already interested, which kind of requirements? I looked it by asking to me whether it were really enough professional to be discrete on what I had the intention to make with it, but I tried my chance, because I needed to kiss somebody who agreed to be called Céline, and I was to do it at least a third of what I wanted to do with Céline. Until that arrives, I would be satisfied with a whore.

Chapter 11

The professor and the virgin nymphet Escort of luxury

I knew that it was unhealthy to act thus, but I was already with my limit. Kaka was attentive while I spoke.

- I will call you by another name, and I will use sex objects on you, and I want that you beg me to eat you during you call me professor. Kaka: Which are these sex objects? Wait, I will show you. I left the part and I went in my room, where I caught a bag, with anal plugs, whips and grips with nipples. It looked at the whip attentively. Kaka: Will that hurt?

- That depends, I can strike slightly. But if you feel pain, say the-me and I will stop immediately. Kaka: Then, that goes. I called it in my room, and inside the room, I opened a second door, which gave access to my room of sex.

It put its hand on its mouth, then looked at me.

Kaka: You all that on me, isn't this will not use? He asked as soon as he saw the significant amount of objects.

- Not, right what there is inside this bag, and I want to give of it you the most possible description, and if you are discrete on this subject, I will be your faithful customer and I will always pay you the surplus amount.

Kaka: It is not serious, I generally do not speak about my customers with anyone.

- Remove your clothing and made all that I say. It was carried out, being stripped to its red corset. I took off my shirt, then I moved towards it, which was there to await my orders.

- Opens your legs. It opened it and I put my hand on his breeches, tightening his she-cat.

I put my hand in his breeches and I realized that it was not yet ready for me.

- Remove your breeches and keep your opened legs, it removed it, leaving its vagina smoothes exposed.

I touched it again and I masturbated, waiting until its she-cat starts to react to my stimuli, which did not take a long time. I detached his corset and removed it, leaving its large exposed round centres. When it was entirely naked, I decided to start to give space to my imagination. "You will be called Céline, and I will eat you in all possible ways, and I want to hear you groan and in redemander." I noticed that its eyebrows contracted in the name of Céline, but I chose to be unaware of this detail. I took it along on the suspended armchair and I attached his arms and his legs, leaving it large open for me. I adored to see women opening with me, because that returned to me absurdly excited and hard.

I removed the remainder of my clothing, leaving me completely naked. I took a condom which I had put in my pocket, I put it on me, I took the grips with nipples and I put it on it.

It closed the eyes and I could say that it was visually excited, which was a good thing, because then it would not be so surface. Without informing it, I penetrated it hard while making him push the first moaning, then increased my movements, returning and leaving my cock violently. I closed the eyes and I started to imagine Céline even if I listened to Kaka to groan frantically.

- That Celine, groans for me, thus that goes... With each moaning that Kaka gave, I penetrated it more quickly and more extremely. I felt my blood to boil by imagining the pink centres of Celine and her breathing in the bathroom. I inserted my cock inside and outside, imagining his voice to ask some more. Kaka: Cat, I will come, says it of a shot down voice.

- Taste the delicious one, go... It pushed a brutal cry whereas it was twisted, incompetent to release itself from the chair.

I left my cock it and I waited until its breathing is standardized, when it was calmed, I slackened it, drawing it out of the shaft hanger, but I kept the grips with nipples. You put at four legs on this chair, have I says by indicating the chair of X, which was used for the anal sex.

I attached his arms and his calves together, then I went to the case and I caught the anal plug. I chose the medium and I introduced it into his bottom, and she again groaned. Then, I started to mass the she-cat to him, again making it wet.

I put my cock in his entry, and I penetrated, while I took and put the plug of his bottom, I also entered and left his she-cat.

kaka: Oh professor, as it is nice, kisses me more extremely, please professor, eats me extremely. I closed again the eyes by listening to supplications of this bitchy girl who did not even approach a Miss Celine.

She groaned bruyamment like a bitch in heat, then I decided to withdraw the plug, and to put my cock in his bottom, and it is there that she started again to shout, and that left me at the edge of the pleasure. I had a whore of band on cries of pain interfered pleasure.

- Miss Céline, I will tear off you the bottom in the most violent possible way. Then, I put that too extremely, too quickly, and she still said that she was going to come. Then, it started again to be twisted with my cock in its bottom.

I had still not come, but I could not any more retain it, thus, I released it, and its legs trembled, and that returned to me even harder.

- Fuck Celine, I will explode my daughter. If you kneel... She knelt and I took the whip. I struck it slightly, and it let escape a small moaning, then I gave some to him another a little more extremely, and it groaned a little more extremely, then I put more force, and it continued to tremble while groaning.

- Is with you to learn how not to face me. I struck even more extremely and it forever asked me to stop.

- And it is because you are so shameless. It started to shout, asking me to continue, but I stopped whipping it, I removed the condom and put my cock in his mouth.

- My Céline cock Sucks, shows me what you can do with this small mouth, will suck. It posed its mouth over the entire length of my sex and started to suck me.

- I will kiss you all the mouth, Céline. Then, I pushed his head while I left it myself and put it in its mouth. I pushed to his throat during which it coated everywhere. I closed the eyes and I continued to push, more quickly and more extremely.

- Oh Céline, I will come to suck this cock... I poured all my sperm in his mouth and she very drank without leaving only one drop of it. She had the air rascal by looking at me and then I could say that I had not been satisfied.

The desire was always also strong and latent to puff out the good she-cat. The she-cat of Celine and all that its body could give me.

- You can get dressed now. I say while turning the back to him and by taking my clothing to get dressed too. Kaka: I never felt also excited with a customer, you know very well how to take along a woman to the paradise. I looked at it, trying to see a pretense of lie, but it seemed to be sincere.

- You are very hot, I liked your service.

Kaka: You are from now on my preferred customer. Of course that I will do it. In addition to making enjoy more once, I always paid it.

- We go ? I invited it to leave the part and we went to the living room.

- Wait one minute and I will seek your money. A few minutes later, I returned.

- Here, two thousand. I had never paid as much for a whore, but it deserved each centime.

Kaka: Thank you cat. Here my chart, you can call me differently than the agency, I will make you a better price the next time.

I liked his initiative.

- Excel average of fidéliser the customers. I made him a kiss on the cheek and it left joyeusement. Who wouldn't be glad to have all that for 1:00 of good kisses? I am turned over in the gaming room and I very cleaned before all to position back.

The odor of the sex is good only while you have of them, after that, they are not good. Once all was scented, clean and organized, I went to take a shower, feeling me frustrated to want somebody as much, but not to be able to have it, because my ego was too large to lose this war. It needed to ask, it was to beg to have me in it, and I was not going to kiss it as long as it would not ask it by looking me in the eyes.

I knew that it was too proud to also ask it, but I would not yield, but I would do anything so that it is the only one to lose this match.

Chapter 12

The professor and the virgin nymphet To try to be strong

After having spent several minutes under the shower, I decided that it was time to leave the shower and to face reality.

No water could extinguish the fire which devoured me. It was distressing of knowing that I had spent the years to protect my virginity, and to risk to lose it with the profit of somebody who lives with many women, and the worst, it is of knowing that women that it took along to the bed beautiful and were tested.

Which experiments do I have if I never slept with anybody? I lay on my bed, completely naked, and closed the eyes, trying to put to me in the head which I was enough strong to support all this pressure, and which I was not going to become right another food of professor Kyle.

Even while thinking more of not being in his bed, I started to feel my she-cat to betray me.

- Not Celine, stops being weak, you cannot go like that. But the image of him covering my mouth and binding me the hands invaded my spirit without requiring the permission.

I slipped my hand to my she-cat and I started to smooth it, feeling all my excitation to run already in my bottom. I will be my centres, imagining it to bite my nipples.

- Oh, I cannot, say myself I. But my spirit tried me to continue, and I increased the movements, and I groaned gently so that Graca does not hear. I became increasingly excited and increasingly weak.

- I any capacity on me when I think of him, how could I do not have capacity on him if I do not even control myself? I thought. I was almost enjoying when Graca struck with my door and I panicked, putting a cloth on me. Graca: Celine, your parents arrived in advance and asked you to go down.

- I will go down now, Graca. I looked at the clock and I saw that it was still 15:30, which was strange since my parents never arrived also early. I went to the bathroom and I washed myself.

- It was although Graca stopped me, I did already something of insane while thinking of this perverse professor. I say while trying to comfort me.

I threaded some clothing and went down, finding my parents in the kitchen having the breakfast.

Mom: Is hello my daughter, it increasingly difficult for us to meet, sorry not to have dined with you yesterday, how occur the courses?

I do not even like to imagine the reprimand which my mother would make if she discovered that I was not attentive classifies some, and the worst, I would lose my car, my chart and all the advantages which I have, if she knew that I leave my professor, smoothes my she-cat. Mother girl ? You me listenings? Where is your chief girl ?

- Afflicted mom, I have just recalled me that I must revise for an examination which will take place Friday.

Father: Proof of which girl?

- Constitutional Law.

Father: Do you want of the assistance? I still have a few free hours.

- Not Father need, I have all the written contents. Of course, I lied. It was true that there was going to be a test Friday, but I had not written anything, because I was concentrated too much on spites of my professor. Mother: Good, I find that they is although you us leashes not to fall Céline, you are the girl of two lawyers, and you know almost all, you have only to re-examine what you know already. It was right.

I do not know why I have if fear badly of making a success of the test if I know really all the subject. It is this professor who prevents me from thinking correctly. I thought.

- Of mom agreement. But changing subject, why are you here so early today?

Father: We will need to travel during four days. We will be of return Sunday, and you are rather old, you can manage all alone.

- Where do you go ?

Mother: A very important customer had troubles in another city, allons-y to help.

- But do you need to go at the same time ? Father: Yes.

- From agreement, that will go.

Mom: Of course that you will do it, we leave to 21:00, we will pass in your room before leaving.

- It is exact. I am turned over in my room and I wondered what I was going to do, having four days without having to explain the university with my parents.

I remembered that I was to leave with Karen for the weekend.

- I hope that it will not take along a male with it, because for the first time of my life, I go there with the intention to profit and from me défouler.

I took my books and I sat down to study. But the business alone made me think of him.

- Which hell of a man. I reniflé With all the difficulties of the world, I succeeded in studying, and there was really nothing beyond what I knew already. Despite everything, I very read and read again very calmly.

When I finished, it made already night, then I decided to call Karen, to confirm our departure, but its portable sounded.

- This bitchy girl must already give her she-cat to an old rich man. It was the only valid explanation so that it extinguished its cellphone.

I tried to recall half an hour later, and she did not answer.

- Karen Shit, releases this cock. I reniflai by looking at the screen of my cellphone. I thus decided to leave a message, so that she recalls me as soon as she will see it. "I need to speak to you, calls me as soon as you finished kissing." Love, cow.

I lay on the bed and fixed the ceiling. - My life needs really to be occupied. I spent a long moment in existential crisis, when my portable sounded, it was Karen.

- My daughter, do you still have a she-cat? Which Karen delay: Amigaaa, you will not believe it, today, I had the best kisses of my life. Which whore of man. She spoke with euphoria.

- With Eduardo or a customer?

Karen: Eduardo does not even approach this customer, the guy is marvellous, it made me benefit from horrors and even the double of paid me what I gain.

- Of agreement, you can thus pay for our festival of the weekend.

Karen: I will pay readily my friend, I want to celebrate that.

- I also will allow myself to leave the rows a little, my parents will travel and will return only Sunday. I had to move away the cellphone from my ear not to be deafened by the cries of Karen.

Karen: From friendly agreement, now, I will hang up again because I will have to occupy me of another customer today. To kiss.

- Of agreement, another. My parents do not have any idea that Karen earns its living like that, if they knew, they would have interfered with my friendship with it. Mother: My daughter, we leave. If you need anything, do not call, send to me a message. Does he say while entering my room without striking, and if I touched myself? I thought. - Of course mom. I went to embrace it like my father.

Father: Be wary of all, my daughter. They left, and I felt really free for the first time. Not that they were always on my back, because they were not it, but since to be the perfect girl all the time was exhausting. I would have four days to be which I wanted to be.

Chapter 13

The professor and the virgin nymphet Bad mood

I awoke of bad mood. In addition to not being able well to sleep, I must still carry with me the desire contained by Céline.

That made a long time that I did not awake like that, because front, the sex for me solved all, but maintaining that must be the sex with the good person.

- I hope that this girl will not do anything today, or I do not answer for myself. I went to the university, resembling some friends, I crossed the corridors with a serious face, that the students came with the intention to approach me, then they gave up.

I heard only the whispers, and chatterings, as if they were rather discrete so that I do not hear them. "What took to him"? "I do not know, but I bet that I change face quickly, you want to see"?

- Not now, Monique, I say harshly, as soon as I live it to try to approach.

Monique: Jeez Kyle, which bad mood.

- I already said it to you, not now Monique. She wrinkled the eyebrows whereas I tried to join my room as soon as possible. There remained still twenty minutes before the beginning of the course and the room was empty.

I took a deep inspiration, trying not to let escape the anger which I felt against myself to have been enough stupid to become insane she-cat of a girl. Perhaps that if I eat any only once, I will forget it as I forget the others. But not, if I do that, I will show him that I lost.

- Shit ! The sex of yesterday was super, but that did not change anything with this obsession which I started to feel for the body, the odor and even the appearance of Celine. How that would it change?

This body was not it his, and God alone knows how much cocks entered this she-cat yesterday.

Without forgetting that I feel an unverifiable desire to kiss Céline, which I think of being too intimate to do it. But this small mouth must make thousand wonders.

- Whore of shit, not now. I say myself by noticing that my cock answered my thoughts.

- Which little girl cretin, I say a little extremely, trying to deflate a little the anger which I felt.

Celine: I hope that you made not reference to me, professor Kyle, because I am insolente and impolite only with those which deserve it.

She entered the part, vêtue of a short leather skirt, boots and of a white shirt maker grinding. I was about to explode and it needed to move away from me quickly.

- The course did not start yet, and I want to be only Céline, please leave. Just there I say while looking far from his centres, towards the table, thus avoiding my desire sucking it.

Celine: I just will leave my business on the chair of the teacher, I have things more important to make than to sit me here with your midlife crisis.

- I am 27 years old girl. I spoke with anger. Celine: She was unaware of what I said, posed its business on the chair and was diverted, going towards the door to which I saw one of my pupils of the other part embracing it on the cheek.

- Whore, it was right what it missed, this wire of whore who trailed around it. Mr. Céline, come here please. I spoke rather extremely so that she hears.

She looked at me and rolled of the eyes, which made me flipper. She did not obey me, and left with him, and I could not control my anger, and I struck the table extremely.

Hatred consumed me and I wanted to punish it in the most painful possible way. I could not continue it, because my cock was hard, which returned to me even more in anger.

The pupils started to enter the room, and settled, except for Céline. I started to stiffen me, imagining thousand things, as if it were my property.

Whereas there remained only one minute before the course, it entered while smearing the lipstick which it had put, which returned to me insane.

I closed my hand and felt my breath to block itself. It looked at me, as if it wanted to pass a message to me, and made a point of sitting down in front of me, to prove that I did not intimidate it.

- Dumb of dumb.

I wanted to take it by the arm and to require explanations on the place where it was and what it made. I looked at my cock, which did not rest me, quite to the contrary, it jumped almost. I wanted to kiss it, until she asks grace.

As we would have an examination the following day, I had the excuse to re-examine the material of examination. I thus did not have to raise me of table. I knew that these last days, Céline had paid attention to none of my courses, then as I cannot be avenged for it of kissing it extremely, I will fill it of questions which it will probably not make be able to answer.

- Good course, let us pass to the questions. Mr. Céline, whom did establish the constitution of 1787? She addressed a smile snob to me and answered.

Celine: She defined key questions, such as the federal presidential republic, the distribution of the three capacities: executive, legal legislature and, unification of the monetary system and measurement, the creation of the Supreme court and the system of election of the Head of the State and government. Did I strike the professor? Yes, it was right, and I could be sure that it would correctly answer all the other questions that I posed to him, but I was not going to miss the occasion to strike it.

- Very well Mister. Celine, in spite of her impertinence and her impoliteness, is at least studious. All the room started to laughing and its smile snob disappeared instantaneously. But I had just pricked the dog with a short stick.

Celine: It is the least which I can realize, therefore I do not have to open the legs with my professor to have high notes. I am too good to need to go down on this level.

- There, it was not necessary any more so that the caus settles. The part was in disorder after that, the boys showing the girls in the part, the girls being defended, being practically devoted to this indirect charge, while Céline and me we look of a threatening air, as if our war were far from being finished.

Chapter 14

The professor and the virgin nymphet imminent Danger

I do not know which kind of demon seized me, and I had doubts if it would release one day my heart, but while waiting, I was ready to play with the devil. I rose while thinking of the kind of anybody that I would be while my parents would have left.

I opened my wall cupboard and there was many clothing which I had bought myself and which I had never used. Perhaps that this person who decided to take the control of the situation always existed, it is me which tried at all costs to hide it, or perhaps that I sold my heart, at the time when I decided to play the game of unpleasant Prof.

I separated a short leather skirt, then I took an irritated shirt maker who marked my centres well, then I separated a boot low, put tiny breeches string white, put red lipstick, I got dressed and I went to the university. I was ready to show the professor who I was not like the others, and it was committed eating me, just like it ate them, my duty is to make him want of it, so that it can learn that it cannot have all that it wants. As soon as I arrived in the corridor, I was already surprised, because it was not with its sexual partisans.

- Doesn't it come today? I thought. At this point in time I live it a little further, entering the room, with a small detail, his partisans were all in the corridor, but they looked at it by far.

- What occurs here? I spoke gently so that nobody can hear.

I was lost in my thoughts when a guy approached me. "Hello, I am called Luke, and I am sorry to have been so daring, but if you do not have a boyfriend, could you give me your number so that we can arrange ourselves to leave one day?" I analyzed it, basic in roof. It was large, with a well defined body, but nothing too muscular, it was white, with honey eyes color, it was the kind of guy with whom I was accustomed to identifying me. I did not seek a connection, but it would make very well tease Kyle.

I was never the kind of smiling and friendly girl, but at this stage, I needed to be it.

- Luke Hello, charmed to meet you, I am called Céline. Let us go with me in my room, I will leave there just my business, and we will be able to benefit from time that it remains us for better knowing us. It was really excited, and it did not seem to believe that it was so easy.

- The men... it is for these reasons and others that I want them far from me. I thought of seeing it dribbling whereas it tried to dissimulate that it did not look at my centres. I entered the part, even if Luke awaited me outside, and I intended the professor to treat somebody of small bitchy girl.

Thus, I teased it by saying to him that I hoped that he did not speak about me, because I was as that only with those which I deserved. He looked at my centres, diverted the eyes immediately and ordered to me to leave the part, because he wanted to be alone. He had the stressed super air, and I foutais myself some.

- I could say to him to have sexual relationships, since he said to me, the other day, that people are stressed as they do not have sexual relationships. But I have chosen to call old man, because I already knew at which point that disturbs it, as if it would never age really, in one moment, his cock will be tired so much that it will want to be withdrawn early. I thought.

When I said to him that I had to better do than to remain in the room and to endure his midlife crisis, it was annoyed and said that it was only 27 years old. I posed my business on the chair and I left, and Luke soon gave me a kiss on the cheek. Kyle quickly called me.

- Bingo, it had to see it. I thought. I looked at it, and I rolled of the express eyes, to show that I was not mood for him, then I was unaware of it and I left with Luke.

- Then Luke, I do not have a boyfriend, but I do not seek any either, but nothing prevents me from better knowing you. Do you have your cellphone over there ? It left its cellphone its pocket and tightened it to me, and I noted my number in his address book. - It is here.

Luke: I hope that you were not mistaken in number here.

- I do not need to do that, it would be easier for me to not say than all this galère to put the bad number on your telephone. I said while trying to be as friendly as possible, but it was difficult.

Now, let leave to me, my course will start. He again embraced me on the cheek, and I went in the part, and as soon as I entered, I made pretense spread out my lipstick, by seeing the glance of the professor fixing me. I sitted opposite him, just so that it can see that its anger did not disturb me. He lowered the eyes and I had the least impression that it was its cock than he looked at.

- Which guy obscene, it cannot control himself and then comes to give a balance. I thought. He was clearly tended and he looked at me as if he wanted to destroy me planet.

He started to teach his class sitting, which increased my suspicions that he had an erection. As if that were not enough, it started to ask me questions, I knew already which was its true intention, which was to embarrass to me in front of the room as if I were unaware of the contents of it, like a manner of punishing me.

- Ah professor, you are so presumptuous. I thought. I knew all the contents, and when I answered him, it had a little surprised air, it really thought that I was going to fall sick.

As it could not make me shame, it treated me the impertinent one and of impolite, by specifying that the fact that I was studious was the only good thing which existed in me. I could keep it there, and I lost the account of the number of times where I played this same scene in my head, I killed it out of so much in different ways, which it should make more attention before teasing me the next time time. It really does not know until where I can go when I am defied.

When I insinuated that I was not like his other pupils, that it was necessary that I draw aside the legs so that it has an high note, he then could realize of the damage which I could make, he understood that when I am in 'do not move with me, because the danger is imminent.

Chapter 15

The professor and the unverifiable virgin nymphet Anger

- Mr. Céline, I need to speak to you. He says at the end of the course, when he saw it rising. Celine: Afflicted professor, that can be later? It is that I will speak about something with Luke in the other part.

He spoke with the same smile snotty-nosed kid as usually. I felt my blood to boil when it mentioned the name of Luke.

- That cannot be later, Mr. Céline, that must be now. At this time, everyone had left the part.

It looked at me, and I knew already that a bad creation would leave this small mouth.

Celine: Listen to professor, your course is already finished, and I do not have any obligation to give you my time after your course, therefore the conversation whom you must have with me will be for later.

She turned me the back, and I advanced with great strides towards her, and took it by the arm, making it be turned over towards me.

- Celine, does not turn me the back while I speak to you.

Celine: For you, that should continue to be "MISS CELINE", and I do what I want Kyle.

- For you, it is "PROFESSOR KYLE". Celine: Of agreement, professor Kyle, please, let leave to me. I continued to hold it, with an unverifiable rage.

- What did you make with this small shit of Luke before my course? Celine: And since when I owe you this kind of satisfaction professor? He spoke while drawing on his arm.

- I do not want that you would be close to him, you include/ understand? She laughed me with the nose, as if she could not believe what I said.

Celine: Do not be a ridiculous professor, you do not direct me, and I am not one of your puppets to do all that you want, and in connection with Luke, it should not be more idiot that you, after all, it is not him which lives by eating half of the university.

I took it again by the arm and I took it along against the wall.

- Does not tease me Céline, I can be quite worse than than you are accustomed to seeing. She looked me with a hatred mortal.

Celine: Can that be worse than that? Thus, that is to say. I emmerde all the university, but remain far from me.

It pushed me extremely, and succeeded in being released from me, and moved towards the door, when I stopped it again.

- You are in anger, because I ate the majority of it, except you. It stopped and was turned over, looking at me.

Kyra: No the professor. It is you, which all can have them, besides me, and now, you feel threatened by a boy, who can carry out what you could not.

I tightened myself instantaneously by imagining this dumb eating it. It put a victorious smile on its face, turned me the back and left. I did not know how to control the desire that I felt to leave and to draw it from the arms of this small shit.

- Celine, you will see what I do with girls like you. I went to my office, and I took a little time to control my breathing, then I caught my bag and I went in another part, where I would teach the next one run. Luke did not perhaps even eat half of the university, but he ate half of the women who existed apart from this one, I myself saw it embracing several with the same evening of them.

I tried not to think of the anger which I felt towards Céline, and concentrated me on the course, after all, the pupils could not be wounded by this whore of nymphet.

- Hello the guy, as you know it, tomorrow I will apply my test in all the rooms, at different hours, you are the first class, therefore I warn you that is not used for nothing to pass the answers to the pupils of the other rooms, because they are different questions and answers, say I while joking.

And I carried out the revision with them, and I made the same thing in all the courses that I followed during the day.

I taught the two quarters, the morning and the afternoon, but the afternoon was not the every day, as Céline studies the morning, I did not see it the afternoon. After our discussion, I did not see it any more and today was one of the days when I was to teach the afternoon.

At the end of my day's work, I was completely tired, psychologically speaking, not because of the courses, as I was accustomed to teaching them, but because of the fight against my own spirit not to become insane while thinking of Céline and Luke.

- How a 18 year old girl can return to me like that? I say myself while returning at home.

I thought of evacuating my anger by eating she-cat, but with the tests which I was to apply the following day, I had still much work to make.

I returned at home, I took a shower, then I ate a fast collation and I went to print the tests. During this time, I thought of the way of punishing Céline for his audacity earlier.

- I know, I will make him a different test, with very an high level. Of course, at another time, I will pass the good test, and I will not make him evil, but I want to see it well despairing to see a test which it cannot answer.

It will know immediately that does not form part of the contents that I taught in class, and it will look at me, and it will know a little my vindicatory side. To use the proof to be avenged is not even close to what I want to do to him, but other moments ago when she will bitterly regret to be open to this kid of Luke.

I finished printing the evidence, can I sat down in front of the computer and I started to formulate the questions for the examination of Celine, it was an examination on the level of the "Aba", American Association off Lawyers, with contents which it is far from having conspicuous.

When I finished, it was almost 22:00. I took my keys of car and I left to seek something to eat.

I went to the restaurant where I always go. I parked my car and I am assembled. The place if was not crammed, I sat down and I ordered my food, and I noticed beautiful brown who drank a beer alone by looking at me.

I knew this look, it was wild and sexy and full with ulterior motives. To each mouthful which it took, it passed its language on its lips.

I fixed my glance on it, showing that I was interested. It rose, launched me a black look, then moved towards the toilets, was turned over and made me a wink, and I included/understood the message very well.

Whereas my food did not arrive, I decided to make a small round in the bathroom. At this point in time I felt hands to draw my shirt and to take me along inside the cabin.

- Lately, I go much to the toilets, thought I. We were in the toilets of the men and of the guy entered the bathroom right after us. We waited until they finished pissing, then it removed my clothing and started to suck me. I tried to retain my growls, not to risk that somebody enters and hears us. I drew it upwards and against the wall, then, I turned it left a condom my wallet and I put it, I raised her grinding dress, I drew aside a little more his legs, then I inserted my cock against it.

I did not know how to treat a romantic woman of manner, not that a woman as that wants any affection, but if ever I started to leave with somebody, it should have the same sexual desires as me. You should like the brutal and brutal sex.

With each punch that I gave him, she groaned délicieusement. "Faster Punch dog".

- Dog ? It is the first time that a woman calls me thus. I thought. Groan more bitch, will groan.

She started to groan very extremely, I dried herself more extremely and she said that she was going to come, then it was the signal for me to come too. She took a deep inspiration, opened the door and left without same asking me my name.

- It is worse than me. I say by withdrawing the condom and by closing the zipper of my clothing. I washed myself the hands then I went to table and my food arrived two minutes later. The woman was not there any more.

- As it is insane, thought I. I finished dining and I left. It was already too late and I needed to sleep. Eh well, the following day would be very amusing.

Chapter 16

The professor and the virgin nymphet Possessive

When I entered this university, I would never have thought that I would cross what I live, all my life, I crossed institutions where the teachers could not be identified with the students, here that should also be like that, but it is not the case, as long as the pupil did not announce the teacher.

I do not need a diploma to include/understand my rights here, I am clearly persecuted by the professor, but I cannot denounce it.

My body becomes animated when it is there, and I do not know how to move away it from me. I have a need absurd to see it becoming insane not to be able to have me, and even if each part of my being wants it, I do not want to be either one moreover in his unslung network of conquests.

As of the end of the courses, I rose while knowing that it would call me, it is always like that, it always calls me when something or somebody threatens it.

He said that he needed to speak to me, and I asked whether that could be later, because I needed to speak in Luke, but I was not really going to speak with anybody. I know the kind of man who is professor Kyle, they like to have the capacity between their hands, and when another man arrives while wanting the same price that them, they panic.

As envisaged, it did not react well, its jaw immediately stiffened and it said that our conversation could not be delayed.

My best diversion is to push it with end and to show him that he is not my owner. I said that its course was already finished, and for this reason our conversation would be for later, then I turned the back to him to try to leave, but it joined me, took to me by the arm and made to me look at it and required that I do not turn the back to him, and it even called me by my name.

I said to him that I was always Miss Celine for him, and it made the same thing when I called it by his name, it said that he was professor Kyle for me. When I asked him to let me leave, it did not do it, quite to the contrary, it continued to hold me, while clearly making include/ understand at which point it was in anger and ordering even the satisfaction of what I did with Luke before the course. I knew that the fact that I made pretense spread out the lipstick would make him believe that I had embraced Luke, it was the goal, I did not know that it would be annoyed as much at the point to become possessive.

Even if I said that I did not owe him any satisfaction of my life and that I released his hand which held my arm, it said that it did not want to see me around Luke, treating it of small shit.

One of the things which makes a person possessive even more possessive, it is to say to him opposite it does not control anything, and it is what I did, I said that it did not direct me and that I was not as his puppets which did all that it wanted, and who Luke was at least idiot that him, because it was not him which ate half of the university. It began again to me by the arm and took along me against the wall in an intimidating way, and said to me not to cause it, that it could be quite worse than than I am accustomed to seeing.

I felt a crushing rage to consume me by intending it to say that.

I said that if that could be worse than that, then he would eat all the university, but he should remain far from me, I cannot explain what I felt, I know just that I hated to imagine it kissing somebody whom he did not make 'it was me.

I pushed it extremely, I released it vind I walked to the door, ready to leave from there before slapping it, but I was stopped walking when I heard his words, saying that I was in anger that he all ate them. , and did not eat me. I did not manage to believe that it was able to say that to me. I looked at it again and struck it in the most poisonous possible way.

I said that it was him which was in anger because it could all have them, but it could not have me, and it felt threatened by a boy who could obtain what it could not. Instantaneously, it was tightened and I saw hatred in his eyes, then I realized that I had just gained this match.

I could still hear a threat of his share saying that I would see what it would do with girls like me.

For the first time since his meeting with him, I wanted to cry. In fact, the simple fact of imagining it to touch, suck, kiss all the women of this university put to me in anger.

- You want to know? I will concentrate on my studies and I will remain possible further from this patient.

I say while entering the bathroom and feeling my eyes to humidify itself.

I washed myself the face, I recovered, then I went to my next course. As I said to Luke, I do not seek a boyfriend.

The men are not worthy of confidence, they are always in the search of somebody to satisfy their sexual desires, then, they end up leaving. I go very well without one, and I do not need any, not more than I do not need a stupid professor who thinks of being able to remove me a crust.

I do not know how I will react if Kyle holds its promise to be a guy quite worse than it is it already. I returned at home, I took a shower, then I am descended to lunch.

Its voice did not stop resounding in my head, saying to me that was going to be worse, as if it were not sufficient to see it surrounded bitchy girls the every day. I am turned over in my room and I decided to study a little more for the test of the following day, I did not need any, but I think that I made it not to ruminate our discussion.

Late in the afternoon, Karen called me. - Hello cow

Karen: Which voice of defeat is this girl? I wondered whether I were or not to speak about the teacher with it, but it was going to make me shit while saying to me to give him my she-cat, which I would not do. - Nothing, I am just tired to study. Karen: You our plans of Saturday, isn't this will not reconsider? I really did not go there, because I needed to forget this twisted professor.

- Of course that not Karen, I already said that I would do it.

Karen: Good, since I need me saouler, I finished by me beating with Eduardo, and I want to forget that there exists at least for a night.

- And why did you fight? Karen: Because I saw it with a blonde, and when I questioned it, he said that the same right that me, he has it too.

- But it, isn't this is always true my friend?

Karen: It is different Celine, the guys with whom I leave are only customers, and it has already his wife. The day when I will have a boyfriend, it will be alone.

I rolled of the eyes by listening to his absurd comparisons.

- Or you can remain unmarried and continue to benefit from your life.

Karen: Perhaps Ouais, you are right. Saturday, I will have them all.

- Not everyone. Leave mine. Karine: How is that? Celine says to me that it will give her chance to a man. - Not, I say that saturdays only, I will embrace a mouth and it is all. Karen: I have a duty to pay for the best discotheque of California.

- Then all is well.

Karen: I will hang up again now, kisses. I hung up again by thinking that it was more than time for me to let to me a little exceed. And it will be a way for me of forgetting Kyle for good.

Chapter 17

The professor and the virgin nymphet Approve

The day rose very differently of the day before, I were of good mood and nobody would take peace to me, not even Céline, on the contrary, I would take it in peace.

I got dressed calmly, with a smile on my face, by thinking of what it will resemble when it passes the test that I prepared to him.

I took my coffee, I recovered all my businesses, then I moved towards the university.

When I am entered, students me have analyzed before to approach, after what they have received of me yesterday, it was obvious that they would be careful, but when they saw that I was of good mood, they recovered to tease me with their splendid centres, exploding almost.

- I hope that you are ready for the test. I say while walking towards the first part where I would apply the test.

I did not see Celine, because I arrived a little advances some, which was well, not to lose my concentration the morning. This demon does not play plays, it always finds a means of causing me in one way or another, that it is with a malevolent comment, a behavior absurdly sexy or a lipstick which emphasizes its lips.

The bell sounded, and the pupils started to enter and to settle, I waited one moment that everyone is in its place, then I started to distribute the tests.

I sat down on the chair and I revalued the test of Celine, it was absurdly difficult. Time passed, and the pupils finished their tests, and they finished all before the bell does not sound, I believe that they studied all to leave so quickly.

As I had time, I corrected some tests, to reduce my work later, at the end of one moment the bell sounded and I prepared to go in the room of Celine, where I was going to put my plan into practice.

By approaching me his room, I became nervous, which was not normal, because no woman had this capacity on me.

- This girl came to destroy my life, thought I.

I entered the part, and I did not find it, automatically my spirit brought back for me towards Luke and that increased even more my nervousness, but I could not lose control not all to lose.

I sat down and I awaited the second ringing to let the students return in the room, at this point in time it entered, vêtue of a grinding black dress, with a slit with the leg, and I quickly had to divert the glance, in front of my cock became hard and I could not provide the proof.

I waited until it assoie in front of me as usual, but it did not do it, which put to me badly at ease.

I raised the eyes and I saw it with the background, looking at the ground, not taking even the trouble to look at me, which was a strange and suspect attitude. - Either it makes it purposely to annoy to me, or it was annoyed with what I said the day before, I thought.

But I would not crack for his small theater. I took the proof, I put his at the end so that there is no error in giving him, I rose and I distributed it to everyone. As soon as I arrived where it was, it kept the lowered head, not raising even the eyes to look at me.

I posed the test on his chair, turned over me and went to my office.

I did not stop looking at it, waiting the exact moment where it would look at me, seeking an explanation to the degree of difficulty of this test, it read, it seemed very concentrated, but it did not look at me.

I gigotais on my chair, trying to control my frustration not to see it desperate, and at this point in time it took its pen and started to answer.

• How this girl will answer something which she did not study? I looked at it, and it showed different reaction, not heavy breathing, not of side glances, exactly nothing, with share to solve the test as if it knew all.

- Or not, she answers all perhaps badly, thought I. I tried to remain as calm as possible, because I knew that no student of first half of the year could answer these questions.

I passed all the test to look at it, people left and it remained, which returned to me very satisfied, because that meant that it had difficulties.

One moment ago when she stopped writing, she looked at just the proof, but she did not look at me, she remained a long time like that, and I awaited only that despair striking, that she looks towards me, at this point in time she looked around her, as if she analyzed the environment, but she avoided looking at me.

- Of what does this girl think? I did not include/understand his reactions. There was only she and two other students in the room, and it remained only 20 minutes before the test does not finish.

Two minutes later, one of the students left, and five minutes after the first, second left, leaving only it in the part.

• I felt the taste victory to soften it my palate. At the time when the last pupil crossed the door, it rose of its chair and moved towards my office. At this point in time it looked at me, its glance was illegible, it did not show any anger, no fear, nothing.

It stopped in front of my office and deeply looked at me in the eyes. Celine: Do you know the difference between us two professors?

• It is right which I would be professor and who you would be the pupil. I answered.

Celine: Not! The difference between you and me, it is that I study my adversary before attacking it. Here my proof.

It placed the test on my desk and was diverted of me, and I did not have any reaction to prevent it from reaching the door.

I passed his test and I looked at the answers, and I felt my head to turn to 360 degrees. She had answered all, and in the worst case, all went well. There were no errors, the test was impeccable and with direct answers.

At the end of the test, she wrote the following sentence. "Do not underestimate me, professor, I am perhaps worse than you usually see it".

- Ordinary Dumb!

Chapter 18

The professor and the virgin nymphet do not underestimate me

It was clear that the mood of professor Kyle the day before was infernal, But that does not justify that it said what he said to me, and I was always very in anger on this subject, and I would try to keep my distances as I said.

In fact, perhaps that I am it, because nobody forever made me wet my breeches like him, my liquid forever cast on my legs by anybody, and I never touched myself before thinking of anyone.

Of course, I already touched myself, but my spirit made me think of people randomly, not with somebody of specific like professor Kyle.

But even if I know what occurs between my legs, I would not be like the others which do not stop being thrown on him, trying to obtain one second of his attention.

It would not have mine either. As much the anguish to look at it consumes me the heart, as much my conscience must fight against my will.

It can eat all the university and whoever is outwards, as long as I do not become one moreover to attend his bed, comparing me to this kind of futile woman, and without one ounce of self-esteem. Today, it is the test of this idiot, and I studied even what I was not supposed to study, I used all the contents of the study files that my parents gave me.

I left the bed, and I went in my wall cupboard and I chose a beautiful black dress, with a slit with the leg, which made my body very attractive.

I was never concerned with this type of things, the men look at me nevertheless, even in behavior of nun. I am not the kind of anybody who passes unperceived.

I got dressed and I am descended for the breakfast. I arrived at the University a little late. I went to my class, and I had my first course, and I listened like a student good in right. Sometimes, I felt my spirit to want to make a turning, for the proof that I will have soon, but I already learned how to control it.

As soon as the first course finished, I rose front seat and on the back seat, I left there my business and I went to the toilets, before the futile professor does not arrive.

I would not give him space to make me the same thing as it makes me since I am here. "You are in anger, because I all ate them except you", its words resound in my spirit, and each time I remember it, anger submerges me, in an intense way.

When I finished using the bathroom, I went in the living room, and it had already arrived.

I moved towards the chair of the bottom, did not look at it a moment, kept the lowered eyes, and I am sure that he wondered why I had not sat down opposite him, as I had always done. I remained thus until the proof is returned.

It moved towards the place where I had sat and mine tightened me. I thought that it was going to test something, or to make a stupid joke, but it did not do said anything nor. When it was withdrawn and turned over to its table, I looked at it while it had the turned back, and I traversed the vision on all his virile body.

But then, I looked at my proof, before it realizes that I ate it with my eyes. I found it very calm, and I thought perhaps that it tried to solidify me, in the same way that I did it, but I changed opinion as soon as I started to read the proof.

- Which bastard daring. Of course, my parents had already shown me the level of the tests which I was to pass to become lawyer.

I knew that the questions of examination that professor Kyle had given me were questions of Aba. I tried not to show at which point anger consumed me at this time.

Because even if I knew the answer, I saw with which point it would be able to make me evil, and if I did not know the answers, I would be bombarded, all that in the name of his ignited ego.

I took my pen, and I answered, and I very read attentively, therefore there are no errors. So front, I retained myself not to look at it, the desire passed immediately, I make some wanted to move away me from him, and not to never again have to look at it.

- It does not know which I am the girl. I thought. My parents are known never not to have lost a business. They are well-known lawyers in California and elsewhere, and I am only at the university to obtain my diploma.

Of course, I do not know all, there is always something to learn again, but in this test, I would obtain the maximum note.

I finished the examination well before time is not past, but I initially left to him a note to the end of the examination and I waited until everyone leaves the room.

I was not going to let pass this configuration of Kyle without confronting it. I looked around me to see whether there were still somebody in the part, and there remained still two pupils.

One is left, then other is left, and when I realized that the professor and me were only in the part, I passed my test and I moved towards him, and then only, I am allowed to look at it.

I controlled my instincts and my desire for killing it, and I took firm steps towards him, which seemed to study me attentively. When I arrived at his table, I looked it in the eyes and asked to him whether he knew the difference between him and me.

But it was also sufficient than ever. He said to me that the difference was that it was the professor and that I was the pupil.

I answered not, that the difference between us was that I studied my adversary before attacking it. I posed the test on his desk, I was turned over and I left the part.

He did not know me, he did not know that the law, it was my life, and that because it was a dream, I prepare to live it since the 14 years age. He does not know at which point I am worker, devoted and studious, he thinks really which I am as these women that he kisses, which needs to smile to have high notes.

I hope that it included/understood the message which I left at the end of the test. It must learn how not to underestimate me, because in addition to not knowing me, it thinks that it can change me, of working me as it wishes it.

It had only once to touch me, so that it thinks that it could be my owner, that there could be things around me, and that I had the duty to serve it.

- Oh, which hatred. I say while entering the cabin of the bathroom. I let run my tears, trying to attenuate the anger which I felt against him.

- Fortunately that tomorrow, it is Saturday, and I will spend a whole weekend without you to see.

I said myself. I left the bathroom and I washed myself the face. Whoever looked at me would see that I had cried. I supervised the other parts, of back, not to be in the field of view of the others.

Fortunately that nobody asked me anything.

I returned at home, just the remainder. My head hurt me, but my heart was in a manner that it had never been before. It was wounded.

And I knew that for the first time, I had made a large shit. I let myself wrap by a professor who yields with everyone, the kind of man whom I always fled and scorned. I returned at home, I took a shower, changed my clothing and I went to lunch.

Then I am turned over in the room and I tried to rest me. My spirit did not leave me quiet, then I was obliged to take a pill and I slept all the afternoon. I rose, I went to eat something and I realized that Graca had already left.

I thus decided to go to the market to buy chocolate and soda, and when I returned, I ordered a pizza pie. I spent all the night to eat and look at films.

While reconsidering at which point my life was tedious.

Chapter 19

The professor and the virgin nymphet : A descent

It was difficult to keep control and the concentration, to have to live with somebody like Céline.

She was completely different from all the women with whom I slept, without speaking about the intelligence absurdity of this girl.

The only problem, it is that this girl has the capacity to kiss with my spirit, it teases me without having to make effort to do it, it confronts me, and does not lower its guard one minute.

I really thought that I could benefit from his despair, I really thought that to deteriorate its proof would be a good means for it of going down from its pedestal, and to ask me of the assistance, but at the bottom, I think that I want just that it looks at me so that I obtain a little his attention.

It makes me hate it of all my forces, and it gives me also desire of it as I never wanted anybody.

- Shit, which defects do you have girl ? I say by looking at his test and by facing this sentence at the end of the test.

She always repeats the same words that I say, to show herself that she is on the same level as me, to prove that I do not have to be able more that she, and that she can use my same tricks to strike me.

She already succeeded in deciphering my weaknesses, and makes use of it as of a weapon to achieve its goals, and it is frustrating to more be able to control its own cock.

I spent the day to evaluate the tests and to think of his whore of test, if it were able to answer such difficult questions, that was not used for only I give him the good test to be passed. I was in the corridor, directing me towards the carpark when I was approached by Monique.

Monique: Professor Kyle, how did I make a success of your examination?

- I still did not correct Monique. Monique: What do you make this weekend? The lack of creativity of Monique is depressing, to use the test to invite me to leave is irritating.

- I leave with a friend.

Monique: Humm, and do you have place for a friend moreover? Shit, I hate the sticking women, and Monique exceeded the limits, it would be easier for it to say than it wants to be still made kiss by me, than I would regulate the problem immediately so that it leaves me quiet.

- Afflicted Monique, but that made one moment that I did not leave with this friend, it is a trick of brother.

Monique: Damage, I thought of being able to repeat this amount.

I needed really an amount of she-cat to leave Céline my head during a few minutes.

- You came by car? If not, I can bring back for you to the house. She addressed a smile narquois and I to me known that she included/ understood my intentions. Monique: I came by car professor, but I can get into your car now.

We walked and the carpark was empty, but it was not reliable, somebody could be presented constantly.

- Monique, I will now take you along to a place, here on the carpark that will not arrive, and then, I will bring back for you so that you can recover your car.

- They is good. It is gotten into my car and I took it along in a motel to two streets of the university. Before I did not leave the car, it opened my pants and started to suck me. It made run its language over the entire length of my cock, with this extreme mouth, making me sigh desire. We entered the continuation, and it was not long in being stripped, it seemed in a hurry to be made kiss.

I did not want to lose too much time either, I wanted just to return and return to the house. I was removing my clothing when it tried to embrace me.

- Afflicted Monique, it is right sex here, not kisses. She had the disappointed air, but so that a woman receives a kiss of my share, our bond must be rather intense, and there was no intensity between me and Monique or no matter whom of other with which I kissed.

I took it along to the bed and said to him to be put at four legs, it quickly obeyed, after all, it knew already how I acted during the sexual relations. I put the condom and I soon put it in his she-cat.

Monique: Oh professor, eats my she-cat, eats, oh as they is delicious, kisses hard kisses... She was enough bitchy girl while speaking like that, very different from the last time where I very managed beginning with the end. With each push, she groaned more and more extremely.

I began with him claquer the bottom, letting it heal, whereas she groaned of pleasure.

Monique: Strike stronger Kyle, striking stronger and strikes more quickly and I will come. I was not kind to take orders, but I wanted to also come, and Monique was not the kind of woman in whom I liked to invest my time.

- Eh well, benefits from you bitch, I will also benefit from it... I inserted several times in it, more quickly and more extremely, while it shouted, it is there that I thought of this blasted nymphet which did not want to only leave me nor the other of my kisses.

- Unhappy. I spoke with anger. Monique looked at me frightened, not including/understanding anything.

Monique: What is nine Kyle, did I do something of evil? At this point in time I realized that I had spoken aloud.

- Not, kitten, you were perfect. She looked at me curiously, then smiles awkwardly. She was held in front of me and smiled.

Monique: I think that one was too fast this time, changes this condom and come to kiss me a little more.

Really, we had gone quickly, but it was my intention, I wanted just to come and it already arrived.

- I do not have any more time, darling, and I just led you here to comfort you not to be able to leave with you this weekend, now, we must go there.

She seemed to include/understand, and I felt sorry to be such a jerk with her, but it is her which approached me, dying of desire for being kissed, and I just gave him what she wanted.

I deposited it at the university then I returned at home. After having met Celine, it became increasingly difficult to concentrate on the she-cat of the women whom I kissed.

All it with what I could think was the whore of she-cat of Celine, I had never seen it, I had just touched it, but this contact was sufficient to make rock all my sexual life.

Chapter 20

The professor and the virgin nymphet: Shaken

After one night depressing, I ended up sleeping on the settee. I awoke with the ringing of my cellphone and I tried to find it.

When I finally found it, I saw that it was Karen.

- You did not sleep, cow? It is still early.

Karen: It is not early Céline, he is already 10:00, awakes maintaining.

- Oh Karen, you and this insane practice to want to give me orders, get stuffed and lets sleep to me.

Karen: If you do not rise now, I will go over there and will make you fall from the bed Céline.

- What devil, what you want? I said irritated and somnolent.

Karen: You prepare and we will make the hair, the nails and the eyebrows, then we will make this basic shaving of the she-cat.

After all, nobody never knows when the car uses our garage.

- You are insane Karen, I do not know how I can still keep my reason by having you like friend.

Karen: I am the fun of your dull life Céline, I will be there in half an hour. It did not even wait until I say if I want or not, it hung up again immediately not to leave me the chance to refuse.

I climbed to my room by trailing me and went to take a shower. I was hungry, but I would need to eat at the restaurant, because Graca does not work the weekend.

After having taken my shower, to be to me brushed the teeth and to be to me equipped, I caught my cellphone, my wallet, and I am descended to await Karen, which arrived two minutes later.

Karen: Oh not Celine, removes this face of somebody who ate and who did not like and goes up the moral one, today it is the day when one will spend the night to be had fun, and it is necessary to be formidable to leave in general to the club.

- And Edouard? Did you already make peace?

Karen: Not, and I do not want, and I have already an eye on another guy. He is not as rich as Eduardo, but he kisses like anybody other.

Allons-y, because I already took go with the living room. We are gotten into his car, and it put the sound at bottom, and it sang like insane. I would have liked to be more excited, but I all the time think so that this professor cretin made me.

I would like to be able to speak about him with Karen, but its councils on the men are not the best.

We spent all the day in the living room and we had to ask the restaurant to leave our food there.

We made the feet, the hands, the hair, the eyebrows and finally, depilation with wax.

My she-cat was absurdly smooth. It was late in the night when we went to the shopping mall, we went in one of the most expensive stores to buy clothing for the club.

I could not even choose my own dress, because Karen saw one of them and immediately said that it was the ideal dress for me.

The dress was really perfect. They was straps spaghetti, and very out of velvet, very short, with a naked back, and an enticing low neckline. If I leant a little, I could see my breeches.

- This dress is beautiful, but it is too short Karen, I will not carry it.

Karen: Celine, please, your body is perfect, you draw already the attention of the guys who wear long clothing, imagines that you wear this dress, you will create sensation, and the idea is to leave the paths beaten today, then does not leave me downwards.

It was right, I needed to let leave irresponsible Céline a little.

- Of agreement, you gained. I took my chart to buy it, but Céline insisted to pay.

Karen: It is a gift to celebrate this new phase which is yours, because you have only to once do it, to want to do it all the time.

- I will not do anything Karen.

Karen: When I say make, I want to say have fun your square. We went to buy a sandal, and I found perfect, it was black also, with a top with high heels.

I bought earrings, bracelets and a new turn of neck, then Karen deposited me at home by saying that it would come to seek me with 22:00.

- My God, I never left also late. This time, I was to return.

I hope that Karen will not put to me in holes. I went up in my room with the bags and posed all on the bed.

I opened my wall cupboard and I left there pantiessest which I could find.

- If is to cause, then I cause well. The breeches were of a pure black and had only one strap. I did not need to separate from bra, because in addition to not for of requiring, the dress is very naked, and it would have the ugly air if I carried it.

After to have chosen all, I went to the kitchen to prepare me a collation, because I had taken one meal in the course of the day.

Whereas it was only 45 minutes with 22:00, I went to take a shower and to prepare me. I took all the precautions of the world, putting on a bonnet on my hair to prevent them from wetting itself.

I put my breeches, and I looked myself in the mirror, I were extremely hot, I got dressed, I was made a beautiful make-up, I left my hair at a peak, I put earrings, a bracelet and a turn of neck and finally, the sandal.

Karen was right, the dress was incredibly sexy on my body. I liked what I saw in the mirror, it was more than time to grow. My cellphone sounded and it was a message of Karen. "I am right in front of the dog, allons-y"? I took all which I needed and I went to his meeting.

Karen: Whore of shit Celine, even me I would catch you, you are so sexy.

- I hope that I do not regret it. I say while laughing.

Karen: Be insane for you? That will be more the beautiful day of your life until now.

- Where do we go?

Karen: Let us see Skyler.

- For Skyler? Is quite simply the most expensive ballade of California Karen.

Karen: I know, and I bought our tickets in advance because it is so difficult to have them at the last minute.

As soon as we arrived, they looked at our name on the list and quickly found it. They asked to us whether we unmarried or were promised in marriage.

Karen: Very unmarried. At this point in time they gave us a red bracelet.

- What means this Karen bracelet?

Karen: That you are free to embrace the mouth of any person whose bracelet is same color as the tien. The room was full, with electronic music in full rise and many people dancing.

Karen: I bought tickets for zone VIP, but just if, so that we have a place where to remain when we are tired.

He spoke with my ear. I just shook the head. One tried to go to the bar, and I was badgered with each step which I took, I had the impression that the guys saw a meat end in front of them. Karen started to make me drink alcohol to help itself to slacken me more, and that functioned.

I went in the middle of the track and I started to dance, letting me carry by the sound of the rate/rhythm, my body became animated and I closed the eyes, it seemed that anything else did not exist, until I feel a body approaching the mien, I opened the eyes to him, and it was a guy, he seemed to be approximately 20 years old, he was white, large, the eyes clear green, the stiff hair, a true cat.

It posed its body on mine, and I sensualized it with the sound of the music.

- It approached and embraced me, it was a slow kiss, tempting, exciting and I do not know if it were the alcohol which acted, but I was with the angels.

It posed its hand on my back and went down to my buttocks. And before it arrives, I felt somebody to violently draw me from his arms and to take me along in a very dark place.

It was so fast which I could not see who had drawn me.

- Lets leave to me, are insane for you? Let leave to me, bastard. I shouted, trying to release me with the hands of the person of which I could not see the face, I could only feel it, but I realized that it was Kyle as soon as it opened the mouth. Kyle: What do you think that Céline made? With shouted.

- I do not manage to believe in it, you can have only one with my face of them. Who do you begin to draw me like that, like a Kyle animal?

Kyle: How did you let this dumb put the hand on you? he with anger says by catching my hands. I did not see anything, but anger that it felt was obvious.

- Releases maintaining me Kyle, I will not wonder it more.

Kyle: You cannot be in anger if you think that I will let you return on this track of dance.

I felt my blood to boil and I started to fight, trying to release me.

- That devil, you are not my owner. He took to me again by the arm and drew me from some steps, until he opens a door and pushes me inside, where he made rather clearly so that I see it. It carried a Jean and a black shirt, and it was very, very sexy.

I felt my breeches to be humidified immediately. It had fury in the eyes. It locked the door and moved towards me. It leant me towards a billiard table, raised my body and sat above me.

Kyle: How much time do I have to say to you that I do not want that you are touched Céline? Spoke about a threatening tone.

- And how much time will I have to repeat that you do not direct me Kyle? Now, let leave to me, say-I trying to leave the swimming pool, but he did not want to leave me.

Kyle: Can't shit Celine, you measure the rage which I feel, while imagining this dumb you to kiss and you it leashes to cherish you, if I re-examine that, you will pay me expensive you hear me? He spoke between his teeth.

- You think that I am afraid of you? Let us put a thing at light here, professor, when I will leave from here, I will kiss the first which appears, included/understood? When I said that, I had the impression to have slackened a wild lion, which was ready with

to kill me. He lengthened me on the billiard table, removed the safety belt of his pants with a masterly speed and attached my wrists, as he had done the other time with his tie.

- Kyleeee, lets leave species to me cretin. I shouted.

Kyle: Celine, you never saw me in anger. It raised my dress and saw my transparent breeches, and it absurdly became hard. One could see the enormous volume of his pants. My breathing was heavy, looking at it fixing my she-cat with such a desire.

It passed its fingers on my breeches, and I turned myself, on the side, trying to prevent it from touching me, but it gave me in the corner, caught one of my legs, and used its other hand to touch me again.

Kyle: You have already your she-cat very pulpy Céline, you cheeks strong, but you cry when you see me. It pushed back my breeches, putting it all between my large lips, and continued to draw it, making back and forth passes, returning to me absurdly excited.

- Kyle, stops now and lets leave to me. He was unaware of me and removed my breeches, leaving my exposed she-cat.

Kyle: Oh Céline, it is much better than than I imagined. He spoke already while falling into my she-cat, he licked me, sucked me and it was impossible to stop my moanings, I twisted everywhere, trying to retain sperm, but it did not want to let to me move away, he inserted his language in my entry, licking all the liquid which insisted to leave my she-cat, and without being able to control it, I ended up having an orgasm in his mouth.

It looked at me and wiped the mouth in front of me whereas I tried to control my breathing.

- From agreement, you already obtained what you want, now let leave to me.

Kyle: It is not even close to what I want to do to you Céline. But if you want more than that, you will have to beg. He said to release my wrists.

- You are insane if you think that I will beg you to eat me as these whores do it. I say while going down from the billiard table and by lowering my dress.

- Return to me my breeches.

Kyle: I will not return it, maintaining it is with me. You can leave now and return directly on your premise.

I looked at it, completely perplexed in front of his audacity and his audacity.

- Kyle, I leave by this door, and there will be a file of insane men for to do everything with me, I do not need to obey to you to make love, I find that in one half-second.

I approached him, which fixed me already glance and I continued...

- You, on the other hand, you can have any she-cat in front of you, but it is with me that you will think, but that one, you cannot have without me to attach it, me to force, without me to badger, because you know that if you let to me go, making my own decisions, you would not even approach with less than two feet me without I wanting it. Therefore, that which must beg to have something here, it is you.

I walked towards the door, ready to open it, when it gave me a warning. Kyle: Celine, if you do not return at home and that you leashes nobody to touch you, I will show another way of crying, and I to you guaranteed to you that in this way, you will not like that. he says by fixing me with a hatred mortal.

As for me, I looked it with scorn and turned over on the track of dance, without me to trouble about the consequences of this decision.

About the Author

I am Sophie Bocuze, a French novelist born in Lyon in 1980. My love for the words and the stories appeared as of my more young age, and I always knew that I wanted to become écrivaine.

After studies of letters and a passage in school of journalism, I launched out in the writing of novels.

My novels explore topics such as the love, passion, the destiny and the secrecies of family. I like to create complex characters and attaching who evolve/move in situations intense and émotionnellement charged. My objective is to transport my readers in another world and to make them live unforgettable adventures.

When I do not write, I like to spend time with my family and my friends, to travel and discover new cultures. I great am also impassioned reading and of cinema.

I am in a hurry to share my next stories with to make you and you vibrate at the rate/rhythm my words.